INSTEAD OF DIAMONDS

INSTEAD OF DIAMONDS
Observations on Life

Carla Lane

MICHAEL JOSEPH

LONDON

MICHAEL JOSEPH LTD

Published by the Penguin Group
27 Wrights Lane, London w8 5tz
Viking Penguin Inc., 375 Hudson Street, New York, New York 10014, USA
Penguin Books Australia Ltd, Ringwood, Victoria, Australia
Penguin Books Canada Ltd, 10 Alcorn Avenue, Toronto, Ontario, Canada m4v 3b2
Penguin Books (NZ) Ltd, 182–190 Wairau Road, Auckland 10, New Zealand

Penguin Books Ltd, Registered Offices: Harmondsworth, Middlesex, England

First published 1995
Copyright © Aromandys Ltd 1995

Typeset in 11/15 pt Monophoto Bembo
Printed in England by Clays Ltd, St Ives plc

The description of Shoreham on pages 176–83 first appeared
in the *Guardian* on 8 February 1995

A CIP catalogue record for this book is available from the British Library

ISBN 0 7181 3904 6

*To the memory of my mother Ivy Amelia
and my father Gordon Di-Vincy Barrack*

I TURN TO THE COMPANY OF ANIMALS

WHEN MY SPIRIT HANGS ITS HEAD

Acknowledgements

My sons Carl and Nigel for always saying wow, great, whenever I attempt the impossible. My brother Ramon and Dorothy. My sister Marna and Leonard; always there. Celia Hammond, fellow protester taking the same path to the same end. Peter, Karen and John, for their constant care of my animal sanctuary. Martine, like minds. N. J. Crisp, dear friend. Bell – my first injured pigeon and the start of it all. And *him*.

Prologue

It is still dark – I am tossing and turning – the grey pillow of my mind is frantic with thoughts, obsessions, things I should have done, things I have done and shouldn't have done, people I should have got to know and understand more – my father, my grandparents, my slightly deranged Auntie Gertie, my first mongrel dog – they have all marched through my head and now they have gone. None of them lived to see my minute success and yet they were all a part of it.

The clock is staring at me and it's raining. My brain just won't let my body go to sleep. Oh God, I hope it doesn't decide to drag me into the future now and dump dismal little blobs of paint on to an already dreary canvas – images of me, bent and sloth-like, gliding among weeping willows with a large flowered hat on my head and a basket full of roses on my arm, wandering in the garden of hopeless causes with cats in my wake and doves in my sky.

I know what's causing this. It was that announcement

on television: 'It is now possible for a woman of any age to have a child, as long as she has got all the relevant bits and pieces.' I rejoiced. Having galloped past fifty, I suddenly felt 'back in the game' – a creature of hormones and ovaries, rescued if you like, from the deep abyss of redundant womanhood. My spirit was felled, however. 'Of course,' said the white-coated, rimmed-spectacled, thin-lipped scientist, 'we wouldn't encourage women over fifty at this point.' The door of life was slammed in my face. I could feel the vital parts of me queuing up for their anti-depressants. Nothing left for me to do but spend what's left of the night thinking about death.

I have never felt optimistic about death, which is sometimes described as the greatest experience of our existence. My immediate thought is try telling that to a cabbage just before you cut it in half. With the rain throwing itself at my window and a lone blackbird offering his first brave note, I concluded that out of the theories and hopeful declarations concerning my end, the one I liked best was the fact that most people die peacefully in their sleep. A tiny thread of logic in me, though, pointed out that as I am a very light sleeper I will probably wake up to die!

It is eight o'clock now. I know because my cats have arranged themselves in a 'where's my breakfast?' row beside my bed. Sixteen bright, pure eyes. The sound of doves in the conservatory and the shifting of my awakening lurcher – these are the sights and sounds which I like best to hear. It is something born out of a lifetime of recognizing the privilege of being in their company. I know that my animals do not look at me with awe – I am the provider. Often when I am caught in their gaze, I mistake it for adoration. But that is a human assumption: what they feel for me dwells in my imagination and in the secret well of their minds.

I think I'll put off getting up. I vaguely remember catching some sleep in the middle of a very important thought. I know. I'll ring my sons, they always sound so pleased to hear me. They bought me a Vodaphone for my birthday, and I bought them one for theirs. Now we have endless conversations every day.

'Hi, Momma.'

'Hi, darling. Where are you?'

'I'm just coming up the Allerton Roundabout. Where are you?'

'I'm still in bed – thinking things out.'

'Hey, I've bought a new tape. Listen to this, it'll blow your mind.'

I put the phone beneath the pillow to mask the soul-throttling sound of young men protesting. It goes on for ever, and when it's over I say with alarming skill:

'Wow, great! Send me a copy.'

Sons

Bits of me,
Splintered in a glance,
Going from the house
Like tall gods smiling
With my smile.

Voices reminding me that I am part of a staunchly
united family, and after these sounds – others – my
mother, my brother, my sister, God, I'm restless! I've
finished my series. I need a break – I need a change.
That's it, that was the important thought. A change – a
book – I'll write a book.

Chapter 1

My life seemed to begin with my first dolls' pram, and the proud walk along Yew Tree Lane with the bright pink silk of my doll's dress spread about and her bare feet slightly raised, the way I instinctively knew that real babies looked. My brother, who is fifteen months younger, speeds past me on his new three-wheeler bike – and there is no one else in that quiet, walled road. Badness, as we know it today, had not begun. We were taught to say thank you when a stranger offered us a sweet, and it was considered rude not to say 'hello' to people who smiled at us. Babies lay safely in their prams outside the corner shop, where the cantankerous Mr Jennings patted the butter into meticulous squares and gazed over his spectacles with Fagin-like precision at the brass scales.

My father was a young merchant navy engineer and my mother, only eighteen, loved no one else throughout her life. It was the presence of this electric thing between them that warmed and comforted the atmosphere in which I was to grow up.

By the time I was five years old, certain financial disasters had overtaken us. We had to give up the house in the walled road and move in with my grandparents. They lived in a typical Liverpool street: rows of red-bricked houses with rainbow doors, brass knockers, lace curtains, aspidistras in dark green pots, white stone steps, cats stretching, canaries singing and young dogs copulating joyfully until Grandma came out with her bucket of water.

They were pure and honest times. Women in aprons grouped together and gossiped unashamedly, each one armed with either a brush or a mop or a shopping basket. Doors were never shut. Men shouted and women cried for all the rest to hear, milk bottles rattled, the ice cream man's bicycle bell clanged, skipping ropes hissed and the thin, sharp sound of marbles colliding in the gutter brought about a gutsy cry from the youngest males, who were waiting uncomfortably for their hormones to get into line. Amongst this sat the granddads and the grandmothers, each one placed carefully in a favourite chair outside the front door, each one wearing Christmas slippers, each one with their glazed eyes fixed on the images of how they once were as their grandchildren plunged and laughed in the street.

Grandmother Foran, on my mother's side, was a spirited lady, small and bold with blackberry eyes. She loved flowers, and used to deliberately pull next door's climbing rose tree over the wall into her yard so that she could get the blooms. She loved her little patch of red tiles, high walls, green wooden gate and profuse creeper with its sometimes green, sometimes crimson leaves clutching the wall and half hiding shimmering spiders' webs. The sun always shone in Grandma's yard. My then best friend Jean Cain and I use to sit on the warm, hollowed step whilst Grandma brought us cocoa and fresh white bread and butter. On Fridays, cats took to the shed roofs, grasshoppers sprang on to clumps of dandelions and dogs could be heard barking deep within the houses as wives and mothers and lovers scrubbed and swilled their yards. A river of water and 'Aunt Sally' disinfectant made its way down to the grid at the bottom of the cobbled passage running at the back of the houses, and there a great frothy dome of soap suds gathered. The boys used to stamp and splash and sail their toy boats in the little river whilst the girls would paddle their dolls and primp the crocheted pillows in their dolls' prams.

Grandma was a Welsh Protestant, married to my Irish Catholic grandfather. They each clung to their individual beliefs, but not with venom. The rule was that when the vicar came Granddad would sit behind his newspaper whistling a tuneless tune, and when the priest came Grandma would clean the big black oven. Granddad was the chief chef on the *Britannia*. In those days there was no ban on bringing animals into the country. The back yard and the 'wash house' were always packed with a variety of jungle birds and reptiles, all of which he gave to animal-loving friends. Once he arrived home with the usual crate of bananas and a small monkey. It used to collect the fruit out of the box, climb up on to the wooden clothes rack and throw bananas down at my grandmother. Eventually the whole family had to migrate to the kitchen until Granddad's ship sailed again and he took the creature with him.

Grandmother Barrack, on my father's side, was a rather dramatic lady. She was gentle-voiced and walked with her head in the air. There was always a sense of adventure in the way she dressed and her jet beads used to make a tinkling sound as they clanked against her brooch. When she was young, she was a seamstress for a titled lady in London and, sitting in her attic window, she used to watch a majestic man with his silver-topped walking stick as he passed by each morning. She was seventeen, he was thirty-seven. One day she arranged to collide with him and they were married six weeks later. He was an imposing man and an accomplished artist. Whenever he smoked his cigar he wore his velvet embroidered jacket and matching hat. Looking back, I see now how full his mind was of nature and how angered he was by man's cruelty. Secure with a private income, he chose to become an RSPCA inspector in the days when only the dedicated were enrolled and wore proudly their navy blue uniforms and silver-braided caps. It took him twenty years of travelling to Europe with cattle for slaughter to bully the Government into passing a law providing separate stalls for them. His desk was full of heart-harrowing reports of broken backs and necks; at the end of one letter it read, 'In their short, cruel life these placid creatures had only one thing to look forward to – their final barbaric death.' In his leisure time Grandfather was an art critic for an intelligent newspaper, and this curious mixture of the two passions made him an enigmatic man who spoke brusquely and had difficulty in endearing himself to the young members of our family. And so I toed and froed between them.

In the street everything was relaxed. I could go into the house for lunch wearing my roller skates, but the rules at the table were strict: good manners, no scraping of knife and fork, no reaching across and no talking with my mouth full. The brass cage with a little yellow bird singing hung in front of the window. Nasturtiums climbed up from the border around the yard and found their way between the window frame and on to the top of the cage. My grandmother allowed them to flourish, until eventually the cage was entombed and the bird used to be let out to sing on top of it during the daytime.

Bedtime in the street was unruly. We would all hang

out of our windows and throw things to each other. Jean Cain and I used to dangle paper spiders in front of the kids who were allowed to play out late and they would tie chocolate caramels on to the end of the string for us to hoist up. We used to ask for torches for our birthdays so that we could shine them on each other's windows. At night the street was streaked with moving shafts of light and the still-gossiping women would pause to shout threats to the culprits, but it had no effect.

Grandma Barrack's country house was quite different. It was rooms full of works of art, monogrammed cutlery, table napkins, and windows overlooking the orchards, and cornfields where the great shire horses pulled the plough followed by a silver cloud of seagulls. Instead of cocoa and prayers at night, it was the inspection of teeth and hands and the eventual sinking into a crisp antiseptic bed.

Grandmother Barrack would parcel me up in the starched sheets and deliver a very controlled kiss on my forehead, then Grandfather Barrack would stand like a great monolith at the foot of the bed and, pointing to a portrait on the wall, he would say, 'Well now, young lady, acquaint yourself with your great-grandfather. As a young soldier he slew seven Russians and saved his platoon. His gauntlets are displayed in the Kendal Museum. He was a man of consequence and here you are, running amok all day, with your petticoat hanging and your nose running. See how he looks at you – with grave disapproval, I would say.' I used to go to sleep wondering how my great-grandfather could go around killing people like that.

The advantage of Grandmother Barrack's house was that, although it backed on to the fields, the front overlooked the River Dee. I can still hear the sound of the old fishing boats coming home at dawn, and the raucous voices of the fishermen as they dragged the boxes of fish across the mud and set them down on the beach before going into their house to sleep a deep sleep. I felt a deep sorrow for the fish, it all seemed so wrong, crammed in boxes away from the environment that gave them life. It was this sorrow that drew me towards the boxes and I used to gaze in horror at the gasping catch – young silvery spotted flook, ray fish, crab, a very occasional salmon – all struggling to breathe. First I used to put the crabs in the mud, and as they made their desperate journey to the nearest deep pool I would take the live fish from the top of the pile and carry them to the water.

Mrs Higgins, the fisherman's wife and the mother of seven fishing sons, would come to the edge of the small wall around their house, which was perched on a high mud bank, and hurl her anger at me. Mr Higgins, now in his combinations, would clamber down the bank, and as he gave chase to me all I could think of was his one black tooth and the face which was savaged and scorched by wind and time. He was my personal monster, and I loved nothing more than to annoy him. The chase ended abruptly by the entrance to my grandparents' house. Safely behind the gate, I used to watch him frothing and stumbling towards it, but he never came in and neither he nor his giant sons could confront the long silent stare delivered by my grandfather, who for appearance's sake would gently usher me away; then, as soon as we were out of sight, he also would give chase, beating the air furiously with his stick and bellowing, 'God damn you, you scruffy, troublesome child!' When we reached the water butt, Grandma would come out and she would grasp the back of my sweater and haul me into the kitchen where I was made to sit still for half an hour.

'My other grandma wouldn't do this.'

'Your other grandmother doesn't discipline you.'

'My other grandma is kind.'

'Kindness does not always have the best results.'

Upon reflection, her pale powdered face was always close to smiling, and I never feared her − not like Grandfather, whose natural dignity I mistook for un-friendliness and who put terror into my heart.

One day everything changed. I was seven years old.

Suddenly my father was no longer going to sea. He had acquired a good job in Camell Lairds shipyard. His debts cleared, he was able to take out a mortgage for a house. We were lifted out of our red-bricked world and dispatched to suburbia, a place where polite children played quietly in their gardens, where people spoke differently – 'posh', we called it – dogs were kept on a lead and flowers stood to attention around well-behaved lawns. We were driven to school in my father's new car. At weekends we used to make him drive down the street and our friends stood open-mouthed. Balls stopped bouncing, tops stopped spinning, pinafored women grew silent and the granddads and grandmothers of the street smiled their tired smiles and lifted tawny hands to wave. We had become their Royal Family.

It was a curious, square-looking car with a leather hood and shiny brass lamps, which took us on our family outings. On Saturday nights my brother and I used to lie in our beds staring out at the sky.

'Do you think it's going to rain?'

'I'm going to pray.'

I would leap out of my bed and get down on my knees. 'Please God, don't let it rain tomorrow.'

My brother was silent. Praying was a girl's thing, but like me he wanted us to go out on our Sunday picnic. By six o'clock in the morning we were both pressed against the window again. Mother was already in the kitchen. We could hear the clatter of the deep red picnic plates being packed in a basket and my father singing in the bathroom. By seven thirty the open-topped Ford car would be grumbling its way out of sleeping suburbia to a place unknown in Wales.

On the way we would pick up Grandma Barrack, who brought yet another basket and a little stove. Such excitement, such leaping up and down. Daddy and Grandma Barrack wore their big teddy bear coats, the family uniform. Mother, however, always the rebel, wore linen dresses with matching shoes, long earrings and coloured silk scarves tied gypsy fashion round her hair. I remember my brother's thin legs and how his tiny body used to be enveloped in navy velour and Fair Isle lambswool gloves. My task was to keep his nose from running. For this I was given a large white handkerchief and, being an 'ever so in charge' sister, I continuously harassed him with it.

There seemed to be no one else living in the world except us as we chugged between the mountains. The adults laughed and talked and pointed. Ramon was always asking for a cake or a biscuit and I just longed to hug one of the lambs on the roadside grass. Finally we would sit by a stream. The yellow checked cloth would be spread, bowls of salads, glass dishes with freshly boiled beetroot, a crusty loaf, creamy butter and cherry fruit cake would be laid out. I can smell now the onions and salad cream and the Camp coffee slowly taking over. After the feast, shoes off, clean cold water where things moved and glided and darted. Daddy would make little rafts out of twigs and Ramon and I would bomb them with pebbles. Then in a laughing family scramble, we would heave Grandma Barrack to her feet and escort her to the stream where she would paddle in a very refined manner, rather like an upright Lady of Shalott, her face set in some kind of dream. After this and other adventures – home, red-cheeked and tired with Mother's suntan cream soothing our tingling backs. We would put up the car hood and set off into the magic of black mountains and orange skies, faraway bleatings and the sound of sharp slates now and then falling down into the valley.

No child could have been happier. The simplicity of it seems old-fashioned now – all we had was nature and ourselves.

Family

When I begin to crumble, they make great scaffolding.

1 Grandfather Barrack.

2 Grandmother Barrack.

3 The ugly years of me, aged seven.

4 My father when a young man, Gordon De-Vincy Barrack.

5 Grandfather and Grandmother Barrack with Mother, Ramon and me on one of our days out in the square-shaped car.

6 My mother, Ivy Amelia Barrack.

7 Grandma Barrack, my father, my mother (in front) and a family friend called Bee.

8 My son Nigel and my mother attending my honorary fellowship at the Liverpool Polytechnic.

9 My son Carl and me at Nigel's wedding.

10 De Vona, one of my grandchildren.

Chapter 2

I wrote my first poem when I was eight. It was to my Grandmother Foran when Granddad died. It read:

> Despair not for him,
> Let sadness grow dim,
> And when sweet birds call
> Smile and recall.

Nobody believed I had written it, such self-indulgent precociousness could not have come from a child's mind – but it had. I persuaded my mother to send it to the *Liverpool Echo*, and it won a poetry competition. With the two shillings and sixpence prize I bought a flea-ridden puppy from the market. I was sent right back with it. One of my most indelible memories is the moment of handing that small dog back to the man with the tattooed arms and the cruel voice, and as I lay in bed that night resentment and frustration grew in me and I longed to grow up. I felt like a moth trying to do what the eagle does. My plan was simple: I would get married as soon as possible – and have a dog.

Whilst I was waiting for the dog, I decided I wanted a baby sister. My parents had not planned this – in fact, it was contrary to all their wishes – but up there in my bedroom I knelt to pray the way Grandmother Foran had taught me: 'Please God, send me a baby sister.' Against the odds she arrived just before my ninth birthday. I pushed that pram everywhere – it was grey with a cream silk canopy – and both grandmothers had made pale satin covers and lace pillow cases for it. We headed for the street, where it was parked on the pavement whilst I graduated from climbing the lamp posts with the boys to being ten and meeting Johnny Graham, the paper boy. He was thirteen, with silk brown hair and an elf-like face. His trousers were always held up with an old tie and he wore heavy woollen socks which gathered like leg warmers around his ankles. When someone told my mother that he had kissed me in the old air-raid shelter, she decided to educate me about sex immediately. This was a very brave step to take, for parents didn't talk to their children about it in those days. She took me into the front parlour and closed the door. There was a vase of daffodils between us, and she kept well behind them as she spoke.

'You know about babies don't you?'

'Yes.'

'They grow in your tummy.'

'Yes.'

'Now a baby will only grow if you are married to a husband.'

'Yes.'

'Like Daddy and me.'

'Yes.'

There followed a desperate pause. She straightened my fringe and then looked down at my feet.

'Those socks were clean for school tomorrow.'

'I couldn't find any others.'

'Right.' She got up. 'Now, don't forget what I've told you.'

She left the room.

Armed with this vital information, and now superbly equipped to go off into the great universe, I strode forth. The pain of being eleven years old was unbearable, for with it came the onset of ugliness. My face seemed too small to accommodate my teeth; my already deep-set eyes created a permanent frown and my body was enjoying a spate of inconvenient sprouting. My breasts arrived without warning – tender little bumps which made me walk with my arms folded in order to hide them – and which seemed to poke out deliberately beyond my gymslip and fleecy lined liberty bodice, providing giggles in the classroom and hysterics in the gym. I could not bring myself to discuss these physical

17

intrusions with anybody, even my most understanding mother, and it seemed to me that I was the only one in school stricken with them. They gathered speed daily.

The completed ugliness arrived when I was fourteen. Marna, the baby sister I had so ardently prayed for, was my only friend and too young to notice my imperfections – although she did prod my chest once and for a moment wore an inquiring look, but some childlike insight bade her keep her mouth shut.

I was thick at school, mainly because I hated it. The discipline wearied me. The very sound of Sister Teresa's habit sweeping the floor of the stone corridor sent fear into my stomach, and the gentle Irish voices of the rest always sounded like a hidden threat. The main problem was my mother. She was beautiful, she didn't wear stockings, she had wild dark hair and a gold cross in her left ear – and worst of all she was married to a Protestant. The sisters could not accept her. When she picked me up from the convent, they hissed softly as she walked past. My classmates said that their mothers had told them she wore a gold chain around her ankle because she was a 'prostitute'. None of us knew what the word meant, but it was whispered with shrinking horror.

One day, during afternoon prayers, I heard a new sound in the corridor. It was loud and purposeful. My father had obviously heard these things and he was bringing his anger to the classroom. The door opened

and there he stood, tall and important looking, his
noticeably blue eyes searching for me. Sister Agatha
put up her hands in Sarah Bernhardt fashion. My father
strode past her and wiped the prayer book off her
desk, then he took my hand and towed me out of the
room. In the corridor a lighted candle burned in front
of the Statue of Our Lady. My father blew it out.
Long-robed sisters bustled to safety like marauding pen-
guins and vanished behind closed doors, whilst in total
silence my father ushered me across the play yard,
bungled me into his car and drove me home. The next
day I was enrolled in the Church of England village
school where I spent the final miserable year trying to
be a scholar.

There are other remembered people during my growing up. The old colonel who lived two doors away:
seventy-nine and widowed, he stood at his gate each day
dressed in his tweeds and stalker's hat, and managed his
loneliness by bidding the time of day to passers-by. I was
twelve then, and I used to go and sit on his gate and
listen to the wonderful stories about his army days, but
the thing which stayed with me was something he said
not long after he'd had a stroke. I took him a hydrangea
which I had picked from his own front garden, and
lying there in his large oak bed, with grey hands spread
on the embroidered linen, surrounded by antique clocks

and threadbare chairs, he fixed me with eyes which had grown weary of seeing and said, 'Don't be like me, spending your last hours fretting about the things you didn't do. Just do it, child, do it.' And I do.

There was Uncle Fred, the family black sheep. He was the son of Grandma Foran's first marriage. He wouldn't work, he wouldn't wear his dentures, his trousers were held up by string and he used to go and clean the brasses at Grandma Foran's house for four shillings a week. He was married to Auntie Flo, twice his height, twice his width and she worked in a jam factory. They lived in a council flat over a greengrocer's shop and there was always a tin of condensed milk on their table and a large sweet jar full of sugar. This was not an acceptable way of life for my grandparents, and although they lived in a street they were drowning in pride. I used to ride my bike to Uncle Fred and Auntie Flo's and spend hours sitting in front of a coke fire just listening to them. They had a language I never heard at home.

'Hey Fred, make us a cup of tea.'

'Make your own tea.'

'You're a lazy bastard.'

'I'm going next door.'

'Get us some fags.'

'Get your own fags.'

'You're a mean bastard.'

At this point I would offer to get Auntie Flo's 'fags'

because I knew she would say, 'And get some caramels for yourself.'

My parents didn't approve of my visits. They blamed the lowliness of the neighbourhood, but I knew that Uncle Fred, with his wild curly hair and unshaven face, was something the neighbours must never see. Even my grandmother used to usher him in and out of her house as if he was going to jail, and when Granddad Foran was home from sea she used to watch the back door latch nervously and as soon as it lifted she would rush to Uncle Fred with his tatty jacket, press four shillings into his hand and bundle him into the street before Granddad had time to get into the house.

When I got home I used to ask my mother, 'Why doesn't anybody like Uncle Fred?'

'Because he's untidy, and he won't get his hair cut.'

'Is he poor?'

'He's poor because he's lazy. Grandma has given him two belts but he still uses string.'

'Is he a gypsy?'

'Yes, that's it – he's a gypsy.'

She did not realize that this excuse to end the conversation would endear me to him. After three more years of secret visiting, taking in so much of the raw Liverpool life, Uncle Fred was rushed to hospital with pneumonia and one day, whilst Auntie Flow was having a quick smoke in the hospital toilets, he made a sad little noise and a single tear ran down his cheek. At that age I was not capable of interpreting it, but it stayed in the back of my mind and often much later in my life when I was goaded by unfair fate I thought of Uncle Fred and his tear.

Then there was Auntie Gertie – Grandma Barrack's sister. She married a soldier when she was twenty-six. He was killed by an army truck three weeks later and family rumour had it that the grief had sent her mad. Shortly after the accident, she crept into the church where they were married and stole a gold cuplet from the altar. The scandal circulated the village and the family rocked in shame. My grandma took her sister into her country house and gave her a room of her own. It was small and cold and Auntie Gertie always wore a big teddy bear coat with polished wood buttons. She looked older than she was, probably because she har-boured a great inner sorrow which sat in her pale eyes – immovable. Her grey hair hung in a thick plait down her back. She wore dark brown dresses and no embellish-ments of any kind. Her skin was gently creased. I often wanted to be rude to her, or to laugh at her. But her private smile always outwitted me, so I would leave her sitting there in the old upturned boat which had been made into a shelter at the bottom of the orchard. She always had a wild flower in her hand and never failed to put it in water at the end of the day, and she would rock to and fro, to and fro, but as soon as a bird came down to the ground she would sense it immediately.

'Hello, little bird,' she would say with matchless affection. 'Dear sweet thing, what are they going to do to you? Go somewhere far away, fly safely, dear sweet thing.'

She had the same attitude towards the rats which came from the woodpile, or the wild rabbits which tumbled through the nettles close by. My brother and I used to skit at Auntie Gertie and although Grandmother Barrack chastised us, she never explained why we shouldn't do it. When bedtime came we never really wanted to kiss Auntie Gertie good night. Grandma used to make us walk across the orchard to do this. Sometimes it was getting dark and there she sat in the half-light, her silk voice warning the creatures of the earth against the human animal.

Grandma would call her, 'Gertie, Gertie, are you there? The children are going to bed.'

Auntie Gertie never responded to our kiss, nor did she ever speak to us directly.

'Mind the frogs,' she would say to the air. 'Mind the creatures of the night.'

Now, with wisdom on my side, I feel ashamed of the way we taunted her and I would love to talk to her and hear why the dance that once went on in her bright mind suddenly stopped. She was found dead, sitting upright in her carved, wooden chair beside the bed. On her knee was a little tin box full of pound notes, amongst which was a small coloured picture of a thrush. I never see a thrush without imagining it's Auntie Gertie come to collect her apology.

After Granddad Foran's death, Grandma came to live with us and I remember Charlie, the man who came round the street every Tuesday in his rickety old van. He sold crockery of every kind and clanged a large brass bell to alert his customers. Charlie liked Grandma Foran. He used to bring her flowered plates and gold-rimmed cups. 'There you are, sweetheart, every one sound.' And to prove his point, he would hold a cup in one hand and a plate in the other and tap them against each other like cymbals. Almost every time they would disintegrate and crash on to the step. 'Oh, well,' said Charlie, 'at least we know don't we?', and off he'd go to get another pair. The kitchen shelves were full of painted dishes – roses, daisies, nasturtiums, soup bowls with red berry handles, cheese dishes with little caterpillars or bees for their handles, and dozens of teapots all with the wrong lids. After the deal, Grandma and Charlie would sit together with a pot of tea and one of her lemon cheese sandwich cakes. The house shivered with laughter. Grandma used to bury her tiny face in her hand as old

Charlie strutted around the morning room mimicking some of his customers. They had time and memory and the fear of it ending in common.

Finally, there was Uncle Tom, my mother's brother. He was a tall, bony man with angry grey eyes. His jacket had leather inserts in the elbows and he got around on his historic bike. Uncle Tom spent all his leisure hours writing letters to soap manufacturers. He was obsessed by their apparent insincerity. Even in those days their adverts boasted about 'extra whiteness'. Uncle Tom used to stand in the morning room and read his letters out to us with the passion of a Shakespearian actor.

Dear Sir,

Last year you advertised the whitest washing powder. Shortly afterwards you boasted whiter than ever washing powder. Now you are telling us that your powder is 'a new whiteness'. May I ask of you, Sir, how many kinds of white there are? And if there are still more to come, then all your previous boasts have not been what you made them out to be. How much more of this verbal skulduggery will we have to endure and will you, dear Sir, be including sunglasses in your next packet of 'whiter than all that has gone before' soap powder?

These letters went on for years. I don't remember Uncle Tom ever reading out a reply. So incensed with what had now become a private anguish, he wrote to the Queen. The letter began with, 'Dear Queen,' and when my mother interrupted him to point out that that was not the correct way to address her, his frustration rose and he very loudly, with the tiny vein in his cheek throbbing, accused us of being 'jelly under the hot water tap of a corrupt society'. Then he stormed out of the house and never visited us again.

All these people brought magic into my early life. Their difference erected my mind. I suppose my indigenous sense of humour loved the way they flitted into the perfect and proper existence which the rest of my family tried to uphold and spat at its human flaws. It was summed up in the little weekly ritual when Uncle Fred used to come to Grandma Foran's house to clean the brasses. She would open the front door and her eyes would sweep over her son in a slow, judgmental way and she would say, 'Go round the back.'

At the age of fifteen, with my brother Ramon and my sister Marna both happy in school, my mother allowed her wayward daughter to leave and take a job in a baby linen shop where I sat all day behind the counter writing poetry, pausing only to serve local ladies with babies' bibs and coloured buttons.

It was behind that counter, in the little wooden shop, that my temperament was fashioned. I saw in the faces of the women who came there a kind of despair. I could never quite decide where their discontent lay. Perhaps it was the task of parading children, the intrusiveness of it, the constant demands from the small bonneted humans who wailed outside in their prams or tugged at their mothers' sleeves as they chose their embroidery silks or their knitting wool. Perhaps it was the embroidery silk or the knitting wool itself. It was impossible to imagine how anybody could need either in a world so packed with choice. Perhaps it was simply the burden of being a wife and mother, with dancing days gone and a new horizon which seemed to stop where the saucepans stood. Either way, I knew that one day I would enter this hypnotic prison – and the faces of these inmates helped me to decide that I must eventually get over the procreative hill and claim back a time for myself.

So the poetry turned into articles, the articles into stories – and the stories into all the things which followed.

After the wooden shop, another shop – this time a big store. They offered me a short course then gave me a job in the cosmetic department, apparently because of my 'suitable bone structure'. These new days were spent mixing fine powders and advising wealthy housewives about their make-up. It was less boring than the wooden shop but I sensed another despair. Most of the women were gallivanting along the stony path of middle age, trying to recover their fleeing youth. I knew that everything I had been taught to say to them and to sell to them was a lie. The small talk about quality and colour and shading was for those with eggshell faces, and the more they bought and wore the older their faces would seem. But in they came with their mink coats and Gucci handbags, leaving contentedly with clown's lips and a canopy of desperate blue eye shadow which as they opened and shut their eyes flashed on and off like Christmas lights. After a couple of months, my own face was taking on the appearance of a cheese and tomato pizza, and my false nails were so long that I lacerated everything I touched. Just as I was settling in to this pseudo world, I was called to the office of the staff controller. She told me in ice-cold tones that unless I wore the pink overall supplied I would have to leave the cosmetic counter. Being a Leo and remembering the strictness of school, I picked up my handbag and walked out through the main door.

My father was on a trial run with a ship from the yard where he worked, so I took this opportunity to explore things he would disapprove of. This led me to a factory which manufactured telephones. I was put on the assembly line, my task being to unite the dial with another component. The factory floor was huge, rows and rows of more pink overalls. The sound of machinery mixed with girls chattering and giggling, and Joe Loss struggled to make himself heard through the black speakers at each end of the floor. This was a new atmosphere – a place of dirty talk and crude jokes. My cheeks developed an almost permanent blush, but from it understanding and insight grew. These girls, with their guttural Scouse accents, displayed friendship and feeling in a way I may never have known existed. They talked openly about their lives and their passions. Sometimes they cried or grew agitated, but glinting through was the humour, the little devil in their Scouse soul, the sudden comment which turned pathos into hilarity.

On my second day, a stranger appeared on the floor – a large, oval man with a purple face and eyes which had a kestrel-like quality. The workers didn't look up when he appeared; there was the odd whisper of 'Oh God, look out,' but that was all. He silently walked amongst the assembly lines, his eyes sweeping along and across, missing nothing. Alice, the girl next to me, muttered, 'That's Mr Hardcock – he's the gaffer. If anything goes wrong, you just yell for him, OK?' Within minutes one of the dials refused to link up with the component. I nudged Alice.

'It won't stick.'

'Call him, then.'

I grappled with the dial but it wouldn't click into place.

'Go on,' said Alice, 'that's what he's here for.'

She thrust my hand into the air and I heard my suburban voice calling, 'Mr Hardcock!'

Alice dug her elbow into me. 'Louder,' she said.

I turned into a soprano. 'Mr Hardcock!'

He walked very slowly towards me and gazed down at me like a great big bear.

'It won't stick,' I said pathetically.

His bird of prey eyes scanned the assembly line. Everything was going on as if nothing had happened. Suddenly he thundered. 'I've told you lot − if this happens again, you'll all be sacked. You'll run out of this room like a badger with a scalded arse.' No one looked up, and he raised his voice yet more. 'Do you hear me? Sacked, I said, the lot of you.' He picked up the dial and with a quick movement he readjusted it. Then he slotted it into place and handed it to me.

'Thank you, Mr Hardcock,' I squeaked.

He bent down and spoke into my ear. I could smell garlic and tobacco. 'By the way,' he said, 'my name is Woodcock, OK?' He walked slowly away and then turned. 'Woodcock, not Hardcock, all right?'

Alice was the first to laugh. Then some others, then the entire floor. Alice, in between her guffawing, managed to say, 'We always do that to new ones, you daft tart.'

My father returned home, and soon after I was summoned to the General Manager's office. My heart was somersaulting as I sat in front of his polished desk.

'Miss Barrack,' he said in his upper-class tone.

'Yes,' I said.

He tapped a cigarette on its box several times before lighting it with a silver lighter.

'I knew your grandfather, John Barrack.'

'Oh,' I said.

'Splendid man. We were in the same lodge together. Splendid fellow.'

I felt some relief.

'He was a fine painter too, a gentleman. Yes, without doubt.'

I waited.

'I want you to report to Mr Mason in the drawing office – tomorrow morning will do. I've already spoken to him.'

'Thank you,' I whispered.

'You'll like it there. A nice class of people.'

I walked along the carpeted corridor, knowing that my father, with good intent, was the instigator of this and I felt let down.

The next day I fed hundreds of architects' plans into a machine, stamped them, put them in folders and put them in filing cabinets. The teacups were china, the voices were refined, the laughter had no guts to it. No one mimicked their old man and there was no larking in the washroom. Here was prison – here was me mentally dying. It was time to find myself a husband and get that dog.

Chapter 3

At the age of seventeen, I met and married a ship's draughtsman who was studying to be a naval architect. We met at the ice rink, where he cavorted in the centre with great dexterity and I clung to the wooden barriers with dreams of being Sonja Henie. By now my family were relieved to see me deposited in a potentially safe situation. A week after our wedding, my new husband brought home something he had seen floating in the river. It was a mongrel puppy.

The next dramatic happening in my life was the birth of my first son, Carl. I had observed the slow but precise malformation of my body through heart-shaped glasses. I was in love with my husband then, and, lost in this fever, I longed to litter the universe with little clones of him. When I was only three months pregnant I bought my first maternity smock. It hung on me like a collapsed marquee. I was impatient to fill it – and when I did I went about proudly thrusting my stomach in all directions, believing no one else had ever performed the on-coming miracle.

I was dispatched to the old Victorian hospital, with its dark green tiles and endless water pipes, on a bright June afternoon, and whisked away from my distraught husband and my calmly efficient mother by a very stern matron, whose face was set in stone and who had only two sentences to her vocabulary: 'Now then, come along, Mother, you'll upset the others,' and 'Who did this?' She took me in an iron lift up to the delivery room. There were two other women there, each one in a more advanced stage of labour than I. They thundered about on their high narrow beds, bellowing like bull seals and clutching masks, which were attached to cylinders beside their beds. The shock to my system was immense. It reminded me of the Renaissance pictures in the gallery depicting war and human savagery. My pale satin nightdress was peeled off and I was introduced to a cream calico shirt which opened down the front and would not cover either my physical devastation or those other parts of me which my mother had spent her life teaching me to keep entombed in a variety of impenetrable knickers. I spent three days in that tiny steamed-up room. Four other babies had been born around me before my son decided to head for daylight, and the stern matron had ordered sticking plaster to be put over my emergency bell.

She stared down at me. 'Now then, come along, Mother, you'll upset the others.'

I launched into a long, loud, never-ending, soul-churning – voices from the dead and dying – scream. At one o'clock in the morning a sleepy doctor was called. He peered into me like an archaeologist examining something rather undesirable lying in the dust, then he uttered a rather incoherent order and the entire staff of the hospital homed in on me and yanked my protesting child into the world.

Later, as I lay with glazed eyes in a bed of gore with the doctor stitching me up as he sang 'You wore a tulip', I found myself inventing a condom with a rein-forced hatch at the end which had a built-in siren and a sperm-destructing missile endowed with the integrity of a Jack Russell chasing a rabbit.

Fifteen months later, in that same hospital with that same doctor in attendance, this time to the tune of 'You stepped out of a dream', I was delivered of another son. Technology had arrived. At the foot of each bed a blackboard had been erected and, written in pale green chalk, were the sinister details of the frantic behaviour of my cervix. Fortunately this birth was more ambitious – Nigel shot out so quickly that a goalkeeper would have been more appropriate than a doctor – and there were so few stitches that the sister administered them with the words, 'Yell as much as you like, love, but keep your bum on the table.'

Less than a year after this the bulldozers came. The

Royal Infirmary was demolished and with it went the sounds of stern matrons, disciplined nurses, buckets and mops, old and gentle porters and the first cries of half the population of Liverpool.

There followed a gap of contentment. I had my two sons, I lived in a nice home in a nice road, I had a nice husband and a nice life. My mother, who lived very close, came every day and with the children on their three-wheelers and the mongrel dog continuously herding us together, we visited all the parks, swings, swimming baths and child-orientated places in Liverpool. Over the long summer days, I used to sit watching my offspring – ever conscious of the precious cargo, but never losing sight of the promise I had made to myself. Those laughing days of my mother would be hard to break away from. But each night, when everybody slept, I sat and wrote endless pages of self-indulgent garbage. Compulsion was at its height and so the frustration began in earnest.

During this time I visited a fortune teller. I was attempting to write a book about gypsies and felt that she was relevant. Her name was Kitty, a well-known and much-loved character in Liverpool. She lived in a council flat, high up amidst concrete and steel. The cold corridor leading to her tatty grey door overlooked a place where four roads converged and traffic and people merged together in a great mass of movement and noise. Kitty sat on a disintegrating wicker chair. Behind her on an old leather settee lay her mongrel dog, which appeared to have a large growth on its undercarriage. Kitty saw my concern.

'Don't worry about her, we've sorted it out.' She addressed the dog. 'Haven't we, my sweet?'

There was a tang of staleness in the air. The flat looked as if somebody had emptied a Hoover bag in it. The mugs on the table were stained with tea and coffee, but the yucca plant standing in the sink was green and strong. She lifted her enormous bosom up in the air with both arms and deposited it on the table next to a pack of cards. I heard the money in the big pocket of her butcher's apron rattle as she did this.

'Wot's yer name?'

I decided to use my own name. 'Romana – Romana Barrack.'

'A bit posh, isn't it?'

Then with such clever moves she placed the cards in four neat stacks and, pointing to each one she said, 'Wot's going to happen, wot will happen, wot has to happen, wot no one can hinder.'

I wanted to point out to her that they all meant the same, but she was now spreading the cards out and in order to make room she had to lean back and allow her bosom to drop below the table again. Her hands were pink and fat and her face was round. She pushed words through her full mouth without seeming to open it.

'Pick a pack,' she said.

I did so. She frowned as she studied the cards. The dog began to stretch.

'Shurrup,' she said. The dog went back to sleep.

After some thought Kitty looked right through my eyes.

'How are yer going to get to Manchester?'

'I'm not going to Manchester.'

'Yer are.' She wiped her nose with her arm. 'So how yer going to get there, then?'

She waited for an answer.

'If I do go,' I said.

'Yer are going,' she said impatiently.

'Then I'll drive,' I said.

She sighed loudly. I was obviously a bore. Then suddenly she said, 'Watch yer back.'

'Pardon?'

'Yer back, watch it.'

I was deeply worried, but she didn't pause. 'And don't play with electricity.'

I waited for her to pick up another card.

'About my back, why should I—?'

She didn't let me finish. 'It's up to you, just watch it, I've told you.'

'And the electricity?'

'Don't mess with it.'

She offered me a cup of tea by nodding to the old teapot on the table.

'No, thank you,' I said politely.

She poured the thick, black, cold liquid into a mug and drank it back, saying on the last gulp, 'You're lucky, you know. You're going to sign contracts and I can see money.'

'What kind of contracts?' I ventured.

'All kinds. They're all over the bloody place here.' She was shifting the cards vigorously. 'Don't bother with men – ever.'

I was depressed. 'I'm already bothering with them,' I said. 'I'm married.' She stared at me. 'I'm warning yer – men is useless to you. Take heed, it's what no one can hinder.'

She lifted her gargantuan bosom and felt around in the big pocket. She rattled the money loudly.

'I don't do this for nothing,' she said passionately. 'People come for miles to see me. Last week I had to drop everything and run to my neighbour's place along the passage. I knew she was in trouble – it was what no one could hinder. When I got there she'd scalded her belly with the chip pan.' She waited for praise.

'Heavens, how amazing,' I said, feeling totally inferior.

'Nothing amazing about it. I don't open my gob unless the truth comes out of it.'

Me

Me in various states of content. A word that
fell through the hole in life's pocket.

1 Me snapped by a photographer on the way to the
  divorce court.

2 Maximus – the most noble of dogs – and me.

3 Holland Park – the days of happy affluence.

4 Igor and me at Broadhurst Manor.

5 Me and part of my gang at Holland Park.

6 Wolfgang, my second cat, now sixteen years old,
  and Silhouette, the rabbit.

7 Claremont: house of many happenings.

8 Igor and me taken by Linda at her home.

9 Me doing my thing at Shoreham.

10 House in Holland Park. Bell lived in the
  conservatory at the back.

Before I left I patted the dog. She rolled over and offered her paws to me.

'I hope she gets better,' I said.

Kitty looked at her dog. 'I've seen to it. We'll both get better, won't we, sweetheart?'

I felt a curious sadness washing over me. The squalor, the hopelessness of living in that concrete prison, an old dog sleeping and an old lady counting pennies on an old table. As I reached the door, she suddenly yelled after me:

'And tell your fella to change his bleeding glasses.'

That was when my heart sank. For months my husband had been saying, 'I must change these glasses,' and I had been saying, 'Don't just say it, do it.' I wanted to stay now, but Kitty was already acting as if I had gone.

A few days later I received a letter from the BBC. The very first sketch I had ever sent in had been accepted for television. The recording, it said, would be in Manchester.

Since the day of Kitty I have signed many contracts and there has been money. I plugged the iron in one day and the electric shock actually scorched part of my sleeve. My back is my weakest point, so now I don't touch anything electric and I don't lift heavy weights. As for men: was she right, or is it just me? I heard eventually that Kitty and her dog died on the same day.

Housework. My unfavourite thing. Something that I had to keep going back to whatever else I did. It had no goal, no reward. Someone always spilled the coffee on the table I had just polished or breathed on the windows I had just shone and, after reassembling the beds, scraping the toothpaste off the bathroom tiles and forcing the dog to regurgitate the missing sock, I would dream another dream: that of being a composer, conducting my orchestra of soufflé dishes and non-stick pans with my wooden spoon as they blazoned bubbly music from deep within the Aga, only to watch it dispassionately disappear into the mouths of those in a hurry, those reading a comic, those with their eyes on *Coronation Street* – or to watch it coagulate where it lay in front of those who preferred a Mars bar.

It was so futile. My theory was that if you go in search of a career, you look for something you long to do, something you could excel at. So what was I doing in the kitchen? My sponge puddings had all the qualities of a road block. Things which went into the oven came out bonded to the wire tray, or simply lay there injured. Indeed, some things dematerialized and never came out at all. The only reason my family survived was because a culinary genius brought out those masterpieces which had written across them 'just add water'.

Sometimes – only sometimes – I would actually get my house in order and I would go from room to room gazing at the artistry of it. Everything was shining. No bits of old cake on the carpet, no sign of a dismantled motorbike or the remains of an abandoned jigsaw. Everything quiet and sweet-smelling, with the dog asleep, the cat stretching and marigolds in the windows. But what was it for? Tired husband would come home and ruffle my hair before he trod half the grass verge up the stairs. He would sit on my carefully arranged silk bed to take off his shoes, leave a trail of clothes to the shower then drip his way back to the wardrobe where he would dismantle the day's ironing looking for the blue shirt he liked to relax in. Carl and Nigel would follow: more grass verge, a gathering of grubby friends around the fridge, the race upstairs to watch *Blue Peter*. One day they would be independent of me and I was prepared to wait for freedom which-ever way it came.

The real worry came when my sons were fifteen to sixteen. The days of scooters and biblical hair. Everybody was frantic to be different. It was something I have always condoned and I tried to remember this when I watched them speeding along the quiet suburban road, lopping off the trees with their fifteen-foot aerials. Policemen appeared regularly on my doorstep to give me a résumé of their antics. My husband, now a fully fledged naval architect and a conscientious mason, adorned in a dark silk suit and with a halo of respectability glimmering around him, could not comprehend what was happening. His sons were wearing pink shirts, an absolute sign of homosexuality. He always spoke in oceanic terms so their hair was like 'seaweed' and their general appearance was like 'something one finds washed up on the coast'. I began to dread the noisy confrontations and then afterwards, whilst our sons slept, my husband and I quarrelled far into the night.

Once he took the offending pink shirts and drove off with them, possibly to the Mersey, with which he had an affinity. By the time he returned, our sons had already dyed their white shirts pink. That night we sat around the table in a troubled silence. The three of them played idly with my terrible potato pie and my mashed daffodil cabbage. The family quartet was eroding. I longed to be free to write, my sons longed just to be free and my husband longed for us to be prisoners of his inhibitions. Then came the speech from the head of the table. 'This is my house and in it you will obey my rules.' His gaunt face was set in disillusionment. He knew by now that I was on a lead of cotton and that his children had taken a strange and unfathomable path away from him. I wanted to hold him and perhaps comfort him, but I couldn't because I knew that soon I would want to leave him.

Watching and feeling the disintegration, an idea was born. It squatted in the back of my mind begging to be written. It was eight years later that I picked up a piece of paper and wrote, '*Butterflies* – Number 1 – Series 1 – Episode 1.'

I had joined a writers' circle in the city and there, each Tuesday night, I sat with other would-be writers and we inflicted upon each other our verbal outpourings. Academically I was behind the others, and this frustrated me. My head was full of tiny sparks. It wanted to know things. I was regretting my wasted school days, the days of coming thirty-fourth out of thirty-seven, the days of counting the bricks on the schoolyard wall or of watching the leaves swirling about the milk crates instead of listening to Miss Pickworth in the village school, who spat out her formula for my future with the aid of a blackboard which she kept prodding viciously with a piece of chalk.

In this regretful mood I wrote my first short story. It was told by a dog who lived on a farm and whose bed was beneath the kitchen table. One day there was another pair of feet beside his beloved master's. The story told how he grew to resent these feet and how one day, in a fit of emotional stress, he bit them. After a terrified run out of the house and across the yard, he sat in a barn waiting for his master's punishment. A great build-up led to the master simply saying, 'Come on, lad, it's you and me now.' I sent it off to a magazine, not really thinking anyone would want to read it. A week later I received five pounds and a letter requesting more. Many more stories and a little white sports car later, I was beginning to think that perhaps I was a writer.

My first visit to the television centre was made in 1970 with my dear friend Myra Taylor, whom I had met at the writers' circle. She was Jewish and darkly attractive, and her conversation was intelligent and imaginative. We had written an over the top comedy called *Up, Down, All Around*. Michael Mills, the Head of Comedy, had sent for us and, abandoning our hungry husbands and wayward children, we caught the seven-thirty train from Liverpool to London and by noon we were sitting in that awesome BBC reception area waiting for our names to be called. Stars and celebrities walked confidently through, calling each other 'darling' and ordering endless taxis from the telephone on the desk. Cliff Michelmore came out of the lift and greeted a small group of important-looking men. There was the sound of intellectual murmurs as they acquainted themselves with each other. He smiled briefly in our direction before entering the lift and I knew that from that moment on I would tell everyone that I knew Cliff Michelmore.

Michael Mills sat behind a large oak desk. He had a well-manicured beard and busy eyes. His socks were white and words gushed from him like a burst water main. He was frighteningly honest.

'We can't possibly do this, of course.' He patted our beloved script. 'It's rather like a Chinese puzzle: no story, no structure, no beginning, middle or end. Simply the ramblings of an undisciplined mind.'

Suddenly I felt naked. I tried to pull my skirt down over my knees. I wanted to be back in Liverpool, mopping my blue tiled porch and waiting for my mother to come for coffee.

However, he said, 'There are some interesting phrases in here, and what is more important it made me smile. So go home and write something that will make me laugh.' He delivered a Svengali glare. 'Have you ever shared a flat?'

'No,' we said.

'Then go home and write about it,' he said. 'And quickly, please. Like yesterday.'

We sat on the train that night, wrapped in a bewildered silence. We had no knowledge of what it was like to share a flat or of scriptwriting. The words 'fade up' and 'fade out' were unknown to us. When we reached Stafford I pointed to a dead tree that stood black against a red sky.

'Look,' I said.

'Yes,' Myra said, and the significance of that minute exchange was that we were able to convey to each other a single word – terror! Rising above the terror was the optimism and it was on this journey that I decided to

49

abandon my own name, Romana Barrack, which suddenly seemed a romantic novelist's name, for the shorter, easier-to-say Carla Lane.

Long hard days followed. *The Liver Birds* was being born. Our scripts were miles and miles of debatable dialogue, most of it irrelevant, but here and there something gelled and a series was the outcome. *The Liver Birds* got off the ground with the awkwardness of a young albatross. Our faces were in all the papers – 'The Writing Housewives' they called us. We were too busy being famous to be angry. That came later.

There are many rungs on the ladder of success, and I have paused on each one. The first was that of arrogance. It came after the successful transmission of the first *Liver Birds* series. Myra was always modest, but I became flooded with self-esteem. I believed that what was going on in my head was important and that, if we were going to have a better world, I was to share my platinum thoughts with the masses.

They were happy, naive days. I had bought a small flat in Paddington with my BBC earnings in order to be in London during rehearsals. I fled between the two cities with people at each end to look after the various animals, some of which travelled with me, namely the Irish wolfhound and the rabbit. On my Paddington mornings I slid out of my husband-uncluttered bed and ate breakfast to the sound of Puccini, then I ran in Hyde Park with my dog. After rehearsals I lunched with a friend and bought antique clothes in Kensington Market. Now and then I would go to the script and add another sentence and then, after speaking to Myra for hours on the phone, I would sleep the sleep of the potentially famous.

At this time we were writing *Liver Birds* scripts separately, coming together regularly in either London or Liverpool to co-write others. The stars were being mobbed in the streets so, while they were signing autographs, Myra and I continued to charm the tabloids – and I started looking for a bigger flat.

One morning, as we were embarking on the second series, a grave blow arrived, in the shape of a BBC envelope. Michael Mills had written to say that *The Liver Birds* was not as profound as he had wished – indeed, not as real – so he was considering calling in new writers. In the very same post was a letter from our agent, long and apologetic, but leading to the paragraph which began: 'These things are always hard to say but, quite honestly, I do not think that you have the potential to become scriptwriters for television . . . ' Myra puffed on her cigarette, her confidence in its death throes, while I, still wracked with arrogance, paced the floor blaspheming them all.

Later that night, after watching a play on television

and the brilliance of Jack Rosenthal, Myra looked at me, blew out a mile of smoke and said, 'I'm tired of this. I want out.'

'We mustn't give up,' I said.

'I have a daughter at home,' she said.

'I have sons.'

'Yours are grown-up.'

'Think what we can give them if we succeed . . .'

The little flame of Jewishness flickered. The conflict within her continued for a few days. A few scenes – then she began to doodle on her cigarette packet instead of writing lines, and soon she was back in Liverpool. I felt bereft. It seemed she had taken all the incentive with her. I missed her brightness, her staunch criticism, the endless fun we had together. But safe in my guts was the promise I had made to myself. I had done the marriage, done the children, done the cooking, done the fruitless journey across miles of carpet with that bloody Hoover. I was not going back.

Later, and with much learned, I was on a higher rung – that of humility. I knew as I swept into the BBC lift clutching yet another script that the pale and anxious newcomers sitting in the reception area whispering, 'There's Carla Lane' would one day be doing the same – and I would be forgotten.

Chapter 4

When I Am Old

When youth has gone,
And I struggle on
With my assorted ills
And my potions and pills,
When the breasts you adore
Reach for the floor,
And my tired face
Hangs like lace
In the window of life,
Will you turn away
And think of the day
When eyes shone clear
And silk days were here?
Will mist and memory crowd your head
As we creak and clatter in our lover's bed,
Or will you reach out
And stifle the scream?

It was during the making of *The Liver Birds* that I met *him*. I walked into the wrong office, and there he was. I had always scoffed at the romantic novels where bronzed limbs and long blonde hair played the major roles and besotted characters acted out their love at first sight as if it really happens. And yet, here it was – in real life – a sort of explosion, and as I walked along the corridor towards the right office I knew that everything was going to change.

During the next few weeks we hunted each other down skilfully and subtly. We managed to be where the other might be – never to collide, but simply to parade before each other. By the time we actually got to sit in the same car the fire was burning ferociously. Compatibility, however, was not on the romantic menu. We went on to a life of marathon quarrelling. So on and on we go, on and on, like fighting cocks until one keels over.

By now my marriage was listing badly in a great sea of anger. My sons had grown up and the clever, strait-jacketed man who was my husband could no longer cope with the eccentric me. I had little to recommend me as a wife. I had now bought a house in Holland Park, which in itself brought about more worry and expense. The stress of commuting between the two houses and living two different lives turned me into an on-and-off neurotic heap. It was my habit on these occasions to clamber into the Range Rover with Maximus, the wolfhound, and simply go. I adored London, and on this Sunday morning, I took to its streets for comfort. Rows of cottages in Kew, white trellis fencing and wrought-iron gates, large houses in Richmond, ivy-clad walls, red stone drives, oak doors, Bushy Park with its fallow deer and long, sharp grass and Sheen graveyard where Maximus and I finally sat and drank water from the tap. Before we left, Maximus paid homage in the usual doggy way to a Mrs Ivy Armitage, Beloved Wife of Ronald Armitage, Born December 1784, Died October 1845.

When I got back to my house the phone was ringing. It was *him*.

'Hello.'

'Hello. Where have you been?'

'To a graveyard.'

'What were you doing there?'

'Oh, just thinking.' Long pause while we silently plotted the next move.

'Are you in tonight?'

'Yes,' I said.

'I might call round. Is that all right?'

'Yes,' I said.

I cooked a meal. It was supposed to be an aubergine pie, but it changed its identity in the oven so I threw cheese sauce over it and served it with good old reliable salad. We ate Licorice Allsorts by the fire and watched a play on television.

Later, in the dark comfort of my bedroom, we lit a candle and began to act out the human dilemma – and just as passion was ready to step off the highest cliff, there was a soft scratching sound coming from behind the television. I remembered that I had locked my cats in earlier while the gardener was coming and going. I had also locked the cat tray in, and now Wolfgang was delivering his eager message and covering it with never-ending conscientiousness. At the same moment Maximus – who had with great dexterity sloped into the room earlier and merged with the carpet – was gnawing on the leg of the bed.

'I can't cope with your bloody animals,' he yelled as he searched for his clothes.

'Then go!' I screamed. So he did.

Later, as I lay on my wet pillow, Maximus brought me his bone. He deposited his sticky present in front of my face and trotted down to his bed beneath the kitchen table.

I like sex – perhaps it's the curious mixture of poignancy, drama and nonsense. I suppose in life we need an equalizer, and the greatest of all equalizers is that exquisitely grotesque fiasco we so willingly indulge in. I am thankful to my parents for my stable attitude towards the subject. When I was a child I used to listen to the strange noises coming from their bedroom, and when I asked my mother about them she said, 'You know when Tiff is asleep' – he was the family dog – 'and he sighs and gasps in his dreams, well people do that too.' It was always a comforting sound after that, but when twenty years later I gave my sons the same explanation the younger one looked at me with suddenly old eyes and said, 'You can get babies doing that.'

Life became exhausting. In my mind I was the original slut. My careful upbringing did not include adultery and yet here I was being seen off at Lime Street Station by one man and being met at Euston by another. Shame accompanied me everywhere. I didn't tell a soul, not even my friend Myra. I was constantly going to the mirror to see if this tyranny had landed on my face.

During the daytime I was able to think in terms of, It's my life, I only have five minutes on this earth. I must do what I need to make it bearable. But at night I could only see the faces of those I was deceiving. The immediate means of escape seemed to be drifting in and out of deep sleeps. Finally I went to the doctor with a stress rash on my face. He gave me some little shiny tablets which turned me into a female version of Rip Van Winkle. I glanced on and off trains without a care in my head. It no longer mattered who saw me off or who met me at the other end, so long as they could carry me to my destination and point me in the right direction for the return journey. Scripts filtered out of my brain in between comas and I managed to honour my deadlines. Most of my time was spent in the BBC lift. I kept getting into it and expecting it to know where I was going, and only after several visits to the basement was I able to comprehend the fact that I needed to press a button.

After several weeks of this catatonic state, I weighed only seven stone. My good friend and fellow Liverpudlian Rita Tushingham kept taking me out for pasta lunches, and on the day my divorce was supposed to come through she towed me round Harvey Nichols trying to uplift me with her rare and wonderful humour. At five o'clock I phoned from there to see what the result was and discovered that my husband had withdrawn and that I would have to wait another three months. Rita bought me a sweet-smelling herb pillow and bungled me into a taxi.

'You'll get through,' she said. 'I did.'

Her face looked alight and I vaguely remember admiring her teeth, which always came as a white surprise.

The tablets had become my saviour. When I got into the house and went to search for them, the bottle was empty. I had forgotten to renew the prescription. I charged around the house like a demented burglar, turning out cupboards and drawers, searching for a pill which might have escaped. Finally I fell into bed and prepared myself for a night of anguished tossing and turning.

In the early light, I woke. The room seemed different. My amethyst beads hanging over the mirror sent little purple streaks across the wall. I could see the fine carving on my wardrobe and noticed for the first time how beautifully the little tassels on the lampshade were made. Outside taxis, cars, an ambulance, squabbling pigeons – all clearly happening around me. Nothing was blurred. I was climbing out of the morass. I phoned *him*.

'I feel better.' (Silence.) 'It's me.'

'Heavens, hello me. You sound different.'

'I want to go somewhere.'

'Where?'

'Anywhere.'

'I'll tell you what: you look at the map. I'll pick you up in an hour.'

The tenderness was there, but no words for my hope to cling to. He was just simply there, a sort of romantic Buddha, to be worshipped rather than to be drawn into a conventional commitment. Looking back it was how I wanted it to be.

As I left the house one morning to go to studio, a cat was run over outside. It crawled on its stomach along the road, looking for somewhere safe to die. I ran into the house for a blanket. Someone had flagged down a police car. When I came out again, the cat was lying on the pavement by the sweet shop opposite. The policeman was trying to get its collar off to read the disc. He was wearing huge, black leather gloves. The stricken creature writhed about, hissing at the policeman in between gasping for its breath. I was suddenly blinded by anger and emotion. I don't know what I said, but soon I was sitting on the pavement, gently stroking the cat's head. I removed his collar, which bore no information after all, then I wrapped him in the blanket and waited for the RSPCA, which the police had called. People stepped over us as they came into the shop. They bought their cigarettes and their Sunday papers.

'Oh, poor thing! Has it been run over? Twenty Gold Tip, please.'

His magnificent eyes never left mine. There was a gentle choking sound coming from him, and his body jerked as if he was a mechanical toy winding down.

The shop was full of people now. Apples were being weighed, the weather was being discussed, I could hear the till bell going and, at one point, loud laughter. Something very important was happening to the cat and me: he was dying and because I was seeing his tragedy – and knowing that one day it would be mine – I was making very important decisions about things I must do in my life.

An hour after the accident, just before the van came, he started to purr between the choking. When the attendant took him from me and clumsily packed him into a cat basket, we were still looking at each other. He grew very still and I saw him die before she picked the basket up.

I rushed into the house and spent the rest of the day cornering my eight bewildered cats and hugging them. By the time evening came, they were totally fed up with me. 'Oh God, here she comes with another wet kiss.' Danielle, the tabby, climbed up on to the lavatory cistern to escape me. The rest went rigid when I picked them up.

'I want to tell you about a cat who purred before he died,' I said. They raised their eyes to heaven and requested to go to bed. Maximus, however, noticed my tears and true to form brought me the remnants of his toy bear.

Death on the Road

I don't know what you were,
You're just blood and tissue
On the road,
Neither feather nor fur.

Perhaps you lived
After the first pain.
Perhaps in your animal way you felt hope,
But they didn't stop,
So you waited.
And when they came with the second pain
There was blackness,
And everything carried on as normal after that.

Chapter 5

Now and then the brief return of arrogance. On a particular morning I went into the television centre accompanied by exultation. My script represented yet another fallout of the brain, another golden product of the mind. Oh God, I thought, now I know how the great artists felt. We are of the same ilk. It was only when the man at the main gate said 'Carla who?' and asked me to remove my car from the Director General's parking place that I climbed down from the dangerous pedestal.

In the rehearsal room, there was an obvious crisis. The producer was wearing his very pink face, and he was twisting a yellow pencil between his fingers. Some of the cast were in their places saying their lines; a curtain of doom hung over the rest. The wardrobe man was making coffee in the corner of the room and two other members of the cast were pretending to do *The Times* crossword, but their eyes and ears were homed in on the pending eruption.

'I still think it's wrong,' said the producer.

'I think it's very funny,' said the actress.

The producer's mouth was smiling, but the rest of his face would not cooperate. 'The way you are doing it might be funny, but the audience will be laughing at *you* and not the situation which you are supposed to be in.'

The face of the young actress set. There was a steady little throb in her cheek. The others shuffled about and the star of the show was vigorously powdering her face with a powder puff. She sat in a great cloud of 'translucent silver beige' pretending that she had heard none of it.

'Ah, here's the writer.'

The producer was glad to see me, and I remembered briefly, as I crossed the floor, of the days not long ago when I – the writer – was regarded as a machine which was programmed by nature to 'to digest endless trivia and regurgitate it in the form of a sit com'. I was not welcome in the rehearsal rooms in those days. Writers were regarded as an embarrassment. Stars didn't like being stared at by the bewildered creator when they changed the dialogue, or decided to play the whole thing with an Irish accent. Things have changed now. Writers have decided that writing a script and not being at its rehearsal is like getting pregnant but not having the baby. With the bringing of pathos and reality to comedy, we have stepped on to a respectable rostrum – a place previously occupied by dramatists only.

I confess to feeling a giant power as I approached the doom-laden group. Those enormously outgoing people who hugged me fiercely and called me darling – who filled me with fear in the beginning – were looking to my somewhat fake intellect for guidance.

'When you wrote this line, Carla,' said the producer, 'did you mean it to be accompanied by a grimace or said with poignancy?'

'It is meant to be a poignant line,' I said.

The young actress pouted. The wardrobe man was still standing with the spoonful of coffee poised over the cup. The star sat quietly in the middle of her cloud of face powder. She snapped her bag closed and in an effort to maintain a neutral position she started to polish her wedding ring with the hem of her skirt.

'We're losing a laugh,' peeved the actress.

So bloody what? I wanted to scream, but out of my mouth came a small verbal symphony of praise and understanding.

In the greenhouse of television, there is no room for bleak truth or unguarded honesty. In order to preserve the fragility of one another, we – the unique band of insecure neurotics – must fight silken tongue with silken tongue: producer, through microphone system, to floor manager – 'What is that silly cow doing? She's changing accents again. We've done a world tour, we'll have to do the scene again.' Floor manager to actress – 'It's all right, darling, nothing to do with you. Slight technical fault. We'll go for it again. Oh, don't forget to keep the *accent* – it was wonderful in rehearsals.'

I drove home joyfully. There is something enchanting about those yellow afternoons, when the sun is getting ready to leave and the windows of houses and offices look like gold leaf. A string of pigeons were silhouetted on an arched park gate. They puffed out their chests and leaned against each other, the one at the end having to stretch his foot out to the side to stop the whole lot from falling. A barking dog came out of the park, and they all lifted with a great whirring of wings. For a brief moment it looked as if someone had thrown a handful of black beads into the air. On the way I stopped to check the bank. In those days I simply couldn't bear money hanging around. I would much rather spend it and get myself into a state of broke. The worry of this fuelled the boiler of my mind into creative mayhem. This meant that the results of my work were better. To all these ends every Sunday I brought home half of the local antique markets. I kept running out of rooms – which is why I graduated from bedsit to small flat to bigger flat to house to bigger house to enormous house in seven years. That is why no one can ever find me, why my accountant's biggest nightmare is the thought of me running amok in London with a chequebook.

In the early evenings – at about five thirty, earlier in

the winter – I put my animals to bed. That cats are usually already queuing up outside the summer room, which is where they sleep and where they get their helping of yoghurt. The three parrots go into verbal competition with each other. Daniel, the African grey, is by far the cleverest. He will declare quite clearly what he wants, and at this time of the day the demands are 'I want a peanut' and 'It's bedtime'.

'Night-night, Daniel, kissy, kissy. I L-O-V-E you,' said in a tone which reminds me how sloppy I can be – and still is a great source of embarrassment as it is followed by a laugh which I refuse to believe belongs to me. When I finally cover Daniel's cage, he can become aggressive and says with alarming ferocity, 'Oh, go away, then.' Julius and Igor, on the other hand, have not mastered the art of human conversation properly. They sit gazing at each other and saying in broken English, 'Hello, sweetheart, hello, darling.'

Around this time, the conservatory becomes very busy. Almost three hundred birds are involved in the 'Last Supper'. The newly fledged hover dangerously on the edge of their nests as their parents cluster in a mass of colour around the supper plate. Large and small, weak and strong, act out their personalities and temperaments around the dish. I watch carefully and any tired or non-coping bird is seized and put in a special cage where life is less competitive. These cages are always open, so some of the wiser birds put themselves in when the going gets tough.

The tortoises, Dante and Beatrix, come clonking into the kitchen towards their lamp where fresh salad awaits. They eat together, then clonk into their bed box by the Aga. Rabbits and guinea pigs squeak from the smaller conservatory outside. They are given a handful of muesli each, and their pen is locked. On to the pigeons, which always greet me with ferocious pecks and severe beatings with their wings. Bell, my first rescued pigeon, clings to my hair and peeps into my face. He is always anxious to tell me many things, nodding and gesticulating towards the others. His excitable cooing no doubt unloads all the gossip of the loft, but alas my inadequate human understanding is incapable of interpreting it, and even when the loft is closed and locked I leave him with his head butting the window in an effort to communicate his findings. Dear Bell, he is never unenthusiastic about life, even though people tortured him once.

When finally *The Liver Birds* ended I fell into a catatonic panic. There seemed to be nothing left to say. Beryl and Sandra had done and said it all and their voices still shrieked in my head. *Butterflies* was sitting there waiting for the noise to stop. I kept picking up my pen and trying to get it on paper, but it wouldn't happen. The days turned into too much coffee, too many cigarettes and eventual exhaustion.

I decided to take my mother to Amsterdam and then on to Paris. This, I thought, would give me time to acquaint myself with the characters of *Butterflies* as well as quench my recurring restlessness. We sat in the Dam Square watching the young drug-takers. There was almost a sleepy atmosphere – hundreds of people with hardly any movement. My mother sat quietly with her nose buried in an enormous ice cream and remarked how worn out everybody looked. We moved on to the Van Gogh Museum where she silently stared at his works of art. In between thinking about my script, I offered little bits of conversation.

'He cut off his ear, you know.'

Her face was deadpan. 'Bloody fool,' she said. And as we came out of the building she told a perfect stranger, 'I was doing better than that when I was ten.' And so on to Paris.

My mother liked Paris, because we always laughed a lot when we were there. And although we had an indigenous dignity there was a tiny part of us which enjoyed being sluts, so we headed for the Pigalle and sat brazenly drinking coffee and notching up our conquests. By the time we got to the respectable areas, I was well acquainted with the characters for *Butterflies* and whenever we sat down to eat or stare I started writing a script

Colleagues and Special Friends
During a show we are bound together by creative passion
and the resulting success.
After that some of us win and some of us lose.

1 Nerys Hughes (*left*) and our Elizabeth Esterson, who
   became the second Beryl in *The Liver Birds*.

2 More *Liver Birds*: Nerys Hughes and Polly James.

3 The 'very thin' me with Nerys and Polly after
   receiving our award in 1973.

4 The *Butterflies* people: (*left to right*) Nicholas
   Lyndhurst, Andrew Hall, Wendy Craig and
   Geoffrey Palmer.

5 Jean Boht, a special friend, and me.

6 Paul and Linda McCartney and me at Broadhurst.

7 The Liver building, Liverpool.

8 The *Bread* symbol.

9 The *Bread* people: (*left to right*) Victor McGuire,
   Graham Bickley, Ronald Forfar, Bryan Murray,
   Jean Boht, Nick Conway, Kenneth Waller, Giles
   Watling, Gilly Coman and Jonathon Morris.

on the back of a map of Paris. Sitting on the Champs-Elysées one day, doing just this, it suddenly started to pour with rain. I towed my mother into the nearest cinema and we felt our way to our seats during the middle of the film. Almost as soon as we sat down I knew we were watching *Emmanuelle 2*, and there on the screen the heroine was sitting on a swing indulging in conspicuous self-gratification. My mother's voice thundered around the hushed dark, 'What is she doing?' I took her by the wrist and hauled her out again. The rain was torrential now, so we ran into the next available doorway and sheltered there.

In my mind I was writing all the time. The occasional 'yes', or 'no' or 'do you want a coffee?' kept my mother contented. She loved abroad, it reminded her of the days with my father and she was able to absorb everything in a silent and intense way. As I was about to imagine scene four, I became aware that she was no longer with me. Then I saw her in a shop, which was tucked behind us. She was rummaging in a large bin. The shop turned out to be a sex-aid shop and the bin was full of adventurous condoms. She had found another stranger. He was tall with silvery hair and a sculptured face, and they were laughing together. My mother held up a red spiked condom and dangled it good-humouredly under his nose. They both laughed again and he spoke a lot of French. My mother uttered a string of well-placed *Ouis*, and before I could intervene they had set off together to explore the rest of the stock. Various kinds of rubber phallics were turned into pretend puppets. My mother sported a strangely feathered thing and her French friend headbutted it with an enormous black plastic penis. Then they giggled over some pornographic photographs and finally they shook hands and he left. The innocence of it was unbelievable. It was like watching children and she was grinning devilishly all the way back to the hotel.

On the plane she told me that his name was François, that he was a bank manager and he was going to look out for her the next day.

'How do you know all that?' I asked. 'You can't speak French.'

'When you're my age,' she said, 'there are some things you just know.'

'Didn't you tell him you wouldn't be here?' I said.

'Why should I?' Her eyes glittered and I realized that she was having a much better time than I was.

Within two days of returning home I was in the Head of Comedy's office. I was excitedly telling him about *Butterflies*.

'It's about this woman. She's married to a good and respectable man, but she's lonely. She doesn't like housework and she's not a good cook. One day she goes into a little café and she meets this man.'

The Head of Comedy was fidgeting unhappily.

'They fall in love.'

The Head of Comedy had grown pale and anxious.

I carried on with a more acceptable scenario They have two sons, it's about the gap between adults and their children.'

His head had begun to slowly shake from side to side. My heart went off to the pit of my stomach to writhe, but I continued. There was nothing else in my head, I had to write it. 'Anyway, this man has a chauffeur. Oh, and her husband is a dentist, but he is shy and inhibited.'

Our eyes met in some kind of deadlock.

'I don't think so, Carla.'

'But why? It's how things are.'

'Drama is how things are, not comedy.'

I made a last appeal. 'They don't sleep together – ever.'

'The viewers are not going to like it. We can't take that risk,' he said.

I left the office feeling empty. Maybe with *The Liver Birds* I had experienced a momentary luck. Maybe it was time to go home. Two weeks later I was delivering the unsolicited script of *Butterflies* Number One to the centre. I placed it at the main desk for the attention of the Head of Comedy and left the building at full speed. For the rest of the day and part of the next I kept trying to think of another idea, but all I could see in my mind was a giant Hoover. It stood in the middle of a vast carpeted field. It was plugged into the local power station and in the distance, above the sound of seagulls, I could hear the River Mersey filling up with dirty dishes. Then a knock at my door. A handwritten note. It read: 'Who am I to argue with a butterfly?'

We were soon into rehearsals. I watched the brilliant cast give life to every sentence and throughout a lovely summer of filming in Cheltenham we experienced the rarest times of all – when hard work came together with professionalism and, in between, helpless laughter.

Chapter 6

Guinea Pig

I don't expect them to understand,
After all, you're only a guinea pig,
And I'm standing here – by the cherry tree,
With the hole made,
And the little parcel of your body, clasped.
Didn't we know each other well, little friend,
Didn't we?

About every six weeks I used to visit the family in
Liverpool. In the usual way, they gravitated towards
Claremont, the old Victorian mansion which had been
the setting for the family joys and traumas since 1973
and another asset made possible by *The Liver Birds*. My
mother occupied five rooms there. It was and is a place
of sons and their people, of dogs and cats, of apple trees
and little white rockery stones to mark the graves of the
family pets. But most of all it is a place of children.

They come from every corner – blond, dark, shy, boisterous – a breathtaking collection of eyes and pony tails. As they manoeuvre me from room to room to show me how Irana can play the violin, how Danielle (the grandchild, not the cat) can answer the phone, how Romana (another grandchild, not me) can put her leggings on by hanging on to Pagan, the Irish wolfhound's collar (their Irish wolfhound, not mine), I was reminded that this cacophony of tiny human persons plunged me into the league of 'grandmother' – although the word was never mentioned, mainly because I used to tower over the crib of every newborn uttering the words, 'My name is Carla, not granny or na-na. Should you once utter that word in my direction, I shall banish your toys.' The threat has been very successful, so much so that when Aeneas was four years old I tested him. 'Who am I?' I said. He looked anxiously around the gathered faces for help then, feeling abandoned, he said, 'You're a very good friend of the family.'

My mother, of course their *great*-grandmother, inherited the title 'na-na', so the children were saved from wondering where the missing relative was. Why? you may ask. In truth I don't like the idea of being thought of as old and frail and the next person to go to heaven. The result of this created image was that when I got to Liverpool nobody offered to carry my case upstairs, and when someone's car broke down they sent for me to help push it.

In spite of all this I knew then that the word 'granny' had actually come into my life. I would have to spend my time fighting it off as if it were a ferocious terrier hanging on to my heel wherever I went, and I would have to combine my great love for these unruly intrusions with the miffed feeling that they were coming by the dozen out of the wombs of young and sinewy daughters-in-law, who until their arrival saw me as a competitive contemporary. I realized in full the plight of my mother when at the age of thirty-eight I crowned her 'granny'. After the kiss of approval placed on the little brown wrinkled face of my first son, she immediately rewrote the family history. My newborn became her son, my sister, only ten years old, managed to qualify still as her daughter but I, now eighteen, had become a sledgehammer to her ego, so I was swiftly put into the category of close family friend, and if a probing acquaintance from the past surprised her with the words, 'I always thought you had another daughter', she would with great dexterity announce that I was at boarding school.

I am vaguely aware that proper grandmothers are supposed to revel in strutting around the park pushing the pram full of dribbling baby and chocolate buttons, whilst the real mother spends her days following her own particular star and her nights getting pregnant again. But I, in a frantic attempt to escape the dragnet, laid down rules. Standing tall over the crib with one eye on the little monster and the other on his doting parents, I declared, 'No babysitting of any kind unless you are both deemed to be in a state of unconsciousness – sworn on oath by your doctor and seconded by an independent specialist. Trivial things like flu, coughs, headaches, broken limbs and fits of depression are not valid.' Now are you saying, 'How cold, how cruel'? But I figured that if I were allowed to follow my particular star my eventual demise would furnish them with enough material assets to combat some of life's most excruciating blows, and that at least my existence would have eradicated from their fate the word 'mortgage'.

As they grow, so does the dilemma. Just as I was in the process of masquerading as a reasonably young and adventurous divorcee, some tall youth or well-developed nubile would shout, 'Hi, Gran!' This happened frequently as we were a family who habitually socialized together, and often as I limped back to the dinner table, bravely hiding the fact that my lungs were pleading with my heart for oxygen, I found myself unashamedly plotting long journeys abroad for them.

One day I will have to come to terms with the truth. It will probably be in the morning, in the winter, when with one foot stuck fast in the duvet and the other painfully trying to reach the bathroom, which suddenly seems to be two blocks away, I will cease fighting off the terrier at my heels and accept the fact that when one's children have children you are, no matter how sprightly the body, how war-mongering the mind, irreversibly a 'granny'.

All my very best friends are within my family. *Butterflies* and *Bread* and *Luv* were fired by their company – their triumphs and their innumerable catastrophes. We are held together by a fierce loyalty, at the hub of which is Ivy Amelia Dawn Barrack – my mother. If I were to describe her as 'spoiled rotten' it would be the truth. She sat like a Queen Bee in her safe, warm chamber while the rest of the family cavorted around getting together sums of money to purchase her life's paraphernalia. She had a small, unworried face, which kept its tranquillity throughout every family drama. Her almost black eyes still contained the brightness put there by my father when he was a dishy young Merchant Navy officer. His death at the age of fifty plunged all but her eyes into despair, and it was easily two years before she smiled again. However, now she was the acknowledged wise and wonderful prophet. The onset of her deafness and the slight failing of her memory did nothing towards the downfall of her wicked sense of humour.

'But Mother, I've told you this at least a hundred times.'

'Well, I can't be expected to remember everything, can I? If I could I wouldn't have put the electric kettle you bought on the gas cooker, would I?' Or her very favourite, 'I am *not* deaf, I just can't hear you.'

A truly beautiful, spirited lady who was too vain to wear the numerous deaf aids I bought her and too young-hearted ever to be old.

Liverpool is my special place. It is a city which is both basic and intellectual – the two mixing so well that you feel caught in some other world. The thick, flat accent lends humour to a simple comment, and poignancy to darker observations. If you should fall to the ground in Liverpool, be you pissed or pained, someone will help you up, someone will offer an altruistic hand with the words, 'Are yer alright, luv?'

Arthritic City

I'm getting near you now, Arthritic City,
I can smell the stone caves near the station,
And soon the steel umbrella of Lime Street,
Taxis like rows of black beetles
Taking our Mary there,
Me Dad here,

And Aunty Cissy into the blossoming suburbs,
Away from your cobblestone soul,
Distancing them from the great docks,
Where ships waited, and grandfathers came ashore
    with their spoils,
And as the red brick and the grey stone,
The wrought iron, the slates and the bells grew
    black with time,
The city planners sat in their sterile offices
Planning the cosmetic surgery,
A lift here, a tuck there,
And during the surgical dig
Your guts took refuge in children unborn.

I usually stayed for a week. We had family dinners in
the big brown kitchen – sons, daughters-in-law, brother,
sister-in-law, sister, brother-in-law. It was at times like
this my aloneness occurred to me. My man in the
background suddenly seemed inadequate and I lay in
bed in that big house planning to go out the next day
and lasso the first appropriate male. Then I recalled
those wingless days of marriage, days of: 'Where are
you going?', 'Who with?' and 'When will you be
back?', and I called *him*.

    'Where are you?'
    'I'm in Liverpool.'
    'You didn't tell me.' (Oh, triumphant move!)

'No, it was a sudden decision.'

'Oh, I see.' (I wait for him to ask me how long I'll be there.)

'What's the weather like there?'

'I don't know, it's dark.' (A little private laugh.)

'How long are you going to stay?' (Playing it ice cool.)

'I don't know.' (That's going too far.) 'Well, a couple of days.'

'Do you mean Thursday or Friday?'

'Er . . .'

'Only I'm going away on Friday.' (Smart bastard.) 'I mean Thursday.'

'OK, I'll see you, then.'

'OK.'

'Bye.'

'Bye.' I clamber back beneath the duvet. I am smiling. The game is a draw.

A Sonnet

In the darker days of man, before compassion
   began
To educate his heart, seep into his bones and swell
   his soul
With understanding, there still dwelt love –
Love from the man to the girl – love from the girl
   to the man,

Before compassion began, there was the glance,
The upheaval of sanity, as two bloods quickened
And the sweet flow of calamity began,
Even in the darkest days of man, before all
    reasoning things began,
There was love.

I drove to the rehearsal rooms feeling somewhat elated. *He* and I had decided that when the show was over we would go to Venice. I already had special memories of the place, having spent three days once walking amongst the great pillars and staring unbelievably at the breathtaking structures which flanked the canals and squatted around the squares. Now I was going to share it – and with him.

As I drove into the courtyard of the rehearsal rooms, a man waved to me from the balcony. He was large and smiling, and when he called me I detected an American accent.

'Want to sell me your show?' he asked.

Those words, said with an American accent, are every writer's dream. Outwardly I was very calm, but my mind was already on its way to Coutts to open a dollar account. 'Want to buy it?' I said.

'I sure do.'

The American and I watched the actors and actresses go through their lines. Every now and then the leading lady would stop mid-sentence and rush over to me. 'It's like acting out my own life – I can't believe it.' Then she would dash back to the bewildered co-star and carry on as if there had been no interruption.

I could see as we watched that there was some tension gathering. The producer was wearing his insecure grin and now and then the three would stand in a group and have quiet discussions. At last the producer came to me. 'She feels that the male character has all the funny lines.'

The star erupted into a mass of agitation. 'I'm just the feed here,' she shouted. 'He gets all the laughs.'

I rose to greet the situation. She was shaking inconsolably and waving her Yves St Laurent scarf about. The producer told the others they could have a tea break and after a mass emotional outburst, resulting in the destruction of several BBC plastic cups, I went on to the balcony to rejuggle the script. My American friend gave me his card and talked about going out for dinner. I mentioned Venice and he shrugged his shoulders. 'Maybe your agent will do a deal. I'll arrange for your trip to Los Angeles.' He zoomed out of the courtyard in a chauffeur-driven Jaguar and the thing I couldn't have realized was that his exciting offer was the beginning of a nightmare.

Finally the cast reassembled. I had levelled out the lines so that each lead felt well served with humour. After a quick read of the alterations, I could see that the male star had fallen into a restrained huff and when he sat down he jerked his right foot back and forth. It was fairly obvious that he disapproved of the changes. Within twenty minutes of rehearsal he was on the balcony, quivering violently and delivering an angry speech to himself.

By now the female star was in the toilet crying, and the rest of the cast had been granted yet another tea break. I visited the balcony again.

'How do you think I feel?' fumed the man. 'Just because that silly cow makes a fuss I have my best lines taken from me – and now *she's* getting all the laughs.'

I found myself saying, 'Is this really what a show is about – laughs? What about life? Isn't there room for that?'

'Of course there is,' he spluttered, 'but why me?'

The producer was anxious. We were dealing with big stars here. Their endearing arrogance always poses a threat to every show, and if resentment is allowed to spring up like weeds amongst the roses the six days' rehearsal time can turn into a travesty. With great charm, the producer said, 'Let's sit down and talk about it, shall we?'

The weeping actress was tempted out of the toilet. Half a toilet roll trailed behind her as she dabbed her eyes and patted her fraught brow. As soon as they saw each other fire and earthquake broke out. The producer leapt about with cups of coffee and kept putting a cardigan around the fermenting actress's shoulders to keep her warm. She kept pulling it off, and so he turned to pampering me. Every time there was a lull he would position a comfortable chair behind me, and when I walked away from his offer he feigned a pain in his shoulder which we all ignored. So in desperation he began talking about dogs, because he knew that we all had dogs.

It is at this time I feel for the producer. His task is not only to put together a good show, but to console and pander to the many people involved – to chain emotions to reason and to launch us smoothly and safely from one recording to another.

The programme was finally done, and the audience laughed in the correct places. Its success was due, I think, to the fact that we reverted to the original script.

Venice was basking in a pale yellow light. The bells of St Mark's were striking the air with their deep warm dong and gondoliers cruised up and down the canals, each one with its macho Italian singing 'Solo Mio' accompanied by a small black concertina. Several cats stretched and preened beneath the bridges, pink and gold glittered on the façades of historic buildings – and rising above this the sound of 'us' – *he* and I yelling at each other outside the Church of Santo Stefano.

'I can't help being hungry.'

'You're always hungry.'

'I need food – not like you. I get a headache. Can't we eat?'

'After the church, for God's sake!'

'I've seen hundreds of bloody churches! I feel dizzy.'

He quickly bought a bunch of bananas and thrust them into my hand. 'Here!' As we walked through the great carved door I hurled my final sentence: 'Next time you go on holiday, take a bloody chimp with you!'

That night, in the Hotel Regina, with its beautiful silk sheets, its marble floors, its view across and along the canal, we lay to attention in the enormous bed. Outside, the rest of the human race enthused about life and love. Then a voice in the dark. 'It's no good. I really can't cope with you.'

Being a master of profound dialogue and burdened with the ability to make the universe go into reverse with my repartee, I said, 'Fine.'

We managed two more silent days. Then flew home.

Chapter 7

If You Were Dead

If you were dead
I'd long to see you.
I would wander through yesterday's places,
Aching,
I would carry your face
In my eye.
I would see nothing else,
And all of me would be
Breaking.

If you were dead,
There would be
A death in me,
And I'd feel your touch,
Endlessly.
I would worship your pillow,
And dream in your chair,
I would hug your cat,

Let him sleep in my hair,
But you're not dead,
You are alive,
And I hate you.

It was time to write another series – something different, something which sprang from my northern guts. I was in Liverpool again, visiting the family, and I took my mother for a drive along the dock road.

'Your father loved it here,' she said. We were gazing up at the great gates of the Albert Dock. 'I used to meet his ship.' She pointed to a heap of old tyres. Buttercups had managed to find their way through the mess and had turned the black heap into a yellow wreath. 'We used to kiss each other there, behind the cocky watchman's hut. My father would have killed me if he knew.'

As my eyes wandered across the derelict site, taking in the still-noble grain-storage buildings, the fierce remains of an iron bridge, cobbled patches of yard and stone bollards where brown tattooed men would tie up their big ships, she told me how my father, at the age of seventeen, had run off to sea. They met at a ship's dance two years later and a year after that they were married, with me strenuously on the way. As she spoke, the concept of *Bread* was being born. My mother's gentle flat voice turned into the gutsy yellings of Mrs Boswell, members of my fairly dignified family each took on a raucous image, and the strangest manifestation was that of my Irish Catholic grandfather, who turned into Lilo Lill. Armed with these thoughts I took up my pen again, and because I was sad and disillusioned, and because Venice seemed now as colourful and as passionate as a council bottle bank, the words fell on to the page. By the end of one script, the Boswell family had marched into existence: words flowed, incidents queued up in my mind. I went with them around our wild city, and picked my best verbal flowers.

There are several variations of the 'successful' show. A bad script can be made special by a good cast, a good script can be lost to a wrong cast, but if you have the combination of a good script and the right cast, plus an excellent producer, your only predators are the tabloids and, gifted with the same ruthlessness as a hungry hyena, they waited for the kill.

Curiously enough, it was my own city which struck the first blow. 'Boring *Bread*', 'Lane thinks we're all scroungers', '*Bread* is a flop' they wrote. The rehearsal room was littered with newspapers open on the pages which bore these caustic comments. It was only the second show. The cast were nervous and delivered their lines without conviction. The producer, a devotee of excellence, kept going over and over the script looking for something to blame. The words 'bloody' and 'bastard' were the chosen targets. He came to me with a quiet discretion and ushered me to a corner.

'Do you think perhaps the viewers might be offended by these words?' he asked.

'Why should they?' I said. 'They are everyday words – everybody uses them.'

'Couldn't Lilo Lill shout something a little less chilling than "bastard" through her cupped hands?' he pleaded.

'Like what?' I asked.

One of the cast overheard. 'You silly billy,' he called.

The rest joined in: 'You rascal', 'You bad boy'. The make-up girl gave her rendering: 'You arsehole'. The wardrobe assistant opened his mouth, but the producer sensed that he had lost this argument and put up his hands to stop the oncoming flow of mounting obscenities. 'All right, all right – bastard stays.'

During lunch hour we sat silently. The guts had gone out of the young and untried cast. But Mrs Boswell, played by Jean Boht, who was already the supporting post for all of us, banged on the table with her fist. 'This is excellent television,' she said, 'we are giving our best. Just wait and see – they'll be mobbing us in the streets.' She held up her coffee cup.

'Fuck them all,' said someone. The rest of us joined in: 'Fuck them all.'

Seven scripts later we were the top series. People

were indeed mobbing us in the streets. The tabloids followed the cast wherever they went. The headlines consisted of fanfares of praise and offers were pouring in to the cast. Peter Howitt, who played Joey, was the first to be tempted. It was a grave blow. I had already written four scripts of the next series when I heard he was leaving. I had to write the rest not knowing who was going to take his place. Later I lost Gilly, who played Aveline, Hilary Crowson who played Julie, and Victor who played Jack. It was clear that one by one they were turning into superstars, and the higher you send them the greater the chance of losing them. Finally Ron, who played Mr Boswell, left – and even with the return of unreplaceable Victor, a new and charming Joey and the faithful, much-loved Mrs Boswell at the helm, *Bread* began to bleed to death. The hyenas delivered their final insensitive bite: 'Stale *Bread* is dead – Oh crumbs!' On the next page it was listed as 'Pick of the Week'!

I was growing weary of London. The lovely Holland Park house was feeling wrong for me. I had accumulated several more dogs and cats, and in the specially constructed building my collection of birds had expanded to almost five hundred. Outside I had my rescued sick and injured pigeons, and in an effort to make up for their various injuries I allowed them to breed. Some of my happiest moments were spent watching these much-maligned birds bring up their young, and when it came to setting the offspring free I always felt that I was releasing them into a hostile world where their endearing qualities were unknown and the name most used for them was 'vermin'. Often, as I walked from the park, one would fly on to my shoulder. If it stayed there whilst I got into my car, I took it home again.

Bell was one of those who stayed. I took him to the park several times to free others, but he always came back with me. A far cry from the days when I picked up his broken body and took him home to my conservatory. I did not expect him to be alive the next morning, but there he was – legs straggled, wings dropped, head to one side. He lived in the conservatory for three years. At first the cats used to line up and watch him through the glass, each one fantasizing about the day I might forget to close the door. In time they grew used to him. He became family and sat on my shoulder all the time I was in the house.

With *Bread* nearly over, my private life had turned into a mixture of turbulence and farce. We – that is *he* and I – had rowed in Malibu, Montpelier, a stretch of beach between Los Angeles and San Francisco, the desert in the Nevada Valley, Dodge City, the doorway of a shop in France and almost every lay-by in England.

Most of the problems seemed to stem from my obsession with animals. This man did not relish eating his breakfast with eight cats homing in on his toast and dipping their paws in the milk jug. I had always shared everything with my animals, and when Maximus, conveniently large enough to offer his paw, would more or less disembowel *him* in the process, I used to sit and watch the resulting war dance with little or no understanding.

I suppose the real rot set in when I delivered my explanatory speech during yet another heated argument about the trespassing of my animals about the house. 'You,' I said, 'are mildly ahead of the birds, level with the cats and way behind the dog.'

Maximus knew immediately that I had spoken words of consequential wrath, and he ran to the front door to await the inevitable rowdy exit. For although Maximus hated being a part of trouble, he loved watching it. Rising above the chaos was the fact that I loved this man. It was because of him that I had come to know the secret temples of myself. It was because of him that I had gone through days of colliding with everybody, of getting into the BBC lift and expecting it to know where I was going, of sleeping with the telephone, of sitting on park benches staring at buttercups and of generally turning into a ridiculous, pathetic, adolescent blob.

Go Now

Go now – the way you do,
The angry glare, the helpless stare.
It's nearly done, and one by one –

The reprisals, then the ritual,
Bed – nothing left to do,
Another final fuck.
Go now – the way you do.

I had met Linda McCartney at Chrissie Hynde's house. We were having a get-together of animal-caring people. Chrissie is a straight-talking articulate lady who is totally unafraid of saying how she feels, and who moves about thrusting passion into her beliefs with accompanying arms and hands. We all talked at once, with Chrissie kneeling in the centre of the floor trying to create order. Linda said to her:

'Is that a leather skirt you're wearing?'

Chrissie replied: 'OK, OK, so we each have our boundaries.'

Linda came back: 'It's a dead cow, nevertheless. Just what are we talking about here?'

Chrissie raised her voice: 'We're talking about what we're going to do with the animals. Maybe I'll stop wearing the skirt when we've finished – OK?'

I knew that they would be my friends. Meeting Paul came later.

'So this is our Carla . . . ?'

'Hi, Paul!'

'Come in, luv, have a cup of tea . . .'

And that's how it always is.

With *Bread* on the last lap and flying high, I decided to give it an injection of immortality. I rang Paul and Linda and asked them if they would appear in it.

'You write it, luv,' Paul said, 'I'll tell you then.'

I wrote a scene for Linda, and one line for Paul. A short time later thay came to Liverpool to film it. We sat in a hotel room eating vegetarian food and waiting to be called for action. When we came out of the hotel, a great warmth sprang up amongst the crowd. It is not just the talent or the star image, it is 'them' and how they are. In spite of wealth and fame, they are tethered to their roots. Their children are untainted by adulation, and above all they find time to speak out for the plight of animals – a brave thing to do when you have millions of meat-eating fans. As for Linda, she, like me, carries the pain of knowing what happens in laboratories, in slaughterhouses, in dark corners where dehumanized people earn their living, sometimes their kicks, harming and terrifying creatures which ask for no more than a little space on this planet.

Sometimes in my melancholia I grow impatient with my own kind.

'They don't care, Paul,' I said.

'Listen, our Carla, there are some real good 'uns out there. I can feel them,' he said.

They are dead, I thought. They died with our grandmothers.

My Granny's Bucket

In the cobbled yard, where the sun played
And insects hung like bits of silk
Above the marigolds,
I heard my granny's bucket
As she scrubbed the step and brought it white
    with stone.
The canary sat in its brass cage
Like a perfect powder puff,
Now and then pausing to watch the visiting bee
As it passed between the bars
On its way to the window box.
Soft stirrings, beneath stones, amongst ivy, by the
    old tap,
Things which fluttered and crawled, unmolested,
In the cobbled yard
To the sound of my granny's bucket.

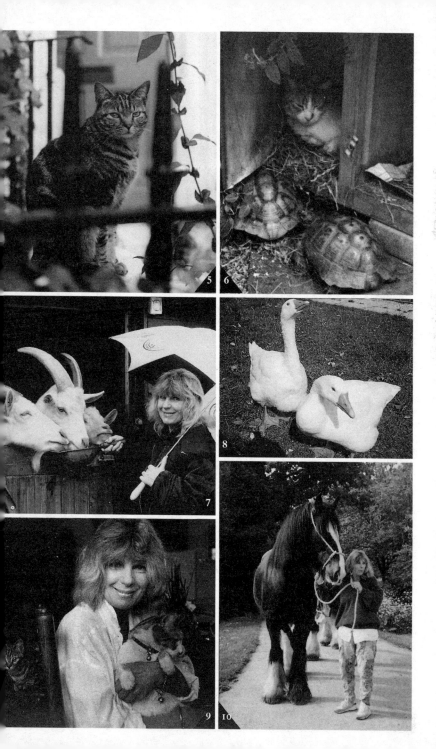

Animals

It all began with a tatty pigeon called Bell.

1 Sorrow – my well-loved cat, died aged fifteen – with Dennis the Cockatoo.

2 The sanctuary.

3 Bell.

4 Joe the crow.

5 Danielle, the cat, strange and mighty.

6 Wolfgang taking over Beatrice and Dante's box.

7 Rescued goats.

8 The sanctuary 'Mafia'.

9 Me with Wolfgang and the sneaky Danielle.

10 Charlie, the rescued shire.

Chapter 8

The American producer had kept his word. My agent rang, my flight to Los Angeles was already booked. 'They want an American version of *Butterflies*,' she told me. No problem, I thought. Los Angeles, here I come.

There was a message on my machine. It was *him*. 'Are you all right?' End of message. I waited until it was late and I was safely established in bed so that, should we have one of our rows, I could grab one of my cats and grieve over it.

'I'm going to Los Angeles.'

'Dear God – what for?'

'They want to do *Butterflies*.'

'Well done, well done.' (Long pause.) 'When?'

'Day after tomorrow.'

'God, that's quick.'

'Yes.'

'For how long?'

'Three weeks.'

At two o'clock in the morning there was a knock on my door.

In the airport we sat drinking coffee and eating big currant buns. I went to buy a film for my camera and came back with one of those silly little plastic cards with the message, 'I love you – sometimes'. I pushed it into his pocket when he was unaware, and when I got to the customs desk there was a little plastic card tucked in my passport holder. It read, 'I love you – sometimes'.

I hated Los Angeles from the moment I stepped off the plane. It was blue and hot and hermetically sealed in an aseptic vacuum. A giant limousine awaited me. It crawled like a big, black caterpillar through palm-infested streets and pulled up outside a hotel which looked like a strawberry gateau. Linen-clad porters carried me and my luggage to a suite overlooking the Hollywood sign and my tall, handsome, blond, slim, full-of-yoghurt driver said he would pick me up the following morning at eight thirty for a breakfast meeting. I lay in the king-size bed gazing at a king-size television and called down for an orange juice. Then the phone rang. 'You're there, then?'

'Yes. I hate it.'

'Why, darling?'

'It's not real.'

'Silly.'

'I want to come home.'

'You've only just arrived. Relax and enjoy it all. Think of the writers who would like to be in your shoes. I mean, it's everybody's dream, isn't it, to be courted by *Hollywood*?'

They arrived with my orange juice. I was glad because it stopped me from saying, 'I love you, I miss you, I don't want to be anywhere without you. Catch the next plane, let's have an argument on a rock in the Atlantic.' I say 'they' arrived, because it took two waiters to push the trolley bearing my orange juice into the room. Their jackets were the same coffee colour as the cloth on the trolley. There was a rose lying beside the glass and in the centre a tall, carved silver object. With lots of 'His' and 'Have a nice days' and 'Gee, you're from Beatle Lands', they bowed their way out of the room. It took me half an hour to dissect the silver container – it was like taking apart a fragile building – and there, entombed in its depths, was a little jug of orange juice. I requested an early call in case they served my morning coffee in an impenetrable catacomb.

Looking through the window of my elongated limousine, I noticed that nobody was actually walking outside. I asked my Adonis driver why, but he was too far away to hear me. We cruised through Beverly Hills and he stopped to point out where Lucille Ball lived. He went on to say that they arranged tours for people to go and see her 'trash can'. We then drove down Rodeo, along

Wilshire Boulevard and arrived at a very grand restaurant. The large, smiling American dismissed the driver and took me to a private room where four other media moguls sat around a huge oval table. Each one shook hands with me and each one began with the words, 'Gee, I'm a great fan of yours.' Silver platters of costly food engulfed me – eggs done every way, bacon, mushrooms, sausages, waffles, bagels, cereal, tea, coffee, orange juice. I chose this moment to announce that I was a vegetarian. There was a sudden halt to the conversation. I quicky broke the stunned silence: 'It's all right, I just love tea and toast. I mean I eat absolutely anything really – except meat.' The man in glasses and a grey silk suit, who turned out to be the chief executive of practically every television studio in America, said, 'Do you eat chicken?'

'No.'

'Fish?'

'No.'

The small shy man with inquiring eyes and auburn-tinted hair asked, 'What do you live on, then?'

It was fairly obvious that he had never entered a supermarket and, like his other colleagues, one darkly handsome, the other blondly so, he imagined that dead animals were the only things available. I chose my words carefully. 'I live on things which don't have to be killed,' I explained, and before they chorused the inevitable 'Vegetables have to be killed', I said, 'That is, anything which is capable of fear and suffering.'

'So how do we know,' said the smiling American, 'whether or not peaches hate being skinned and eggs are terrified of being boiled?'

'We don't,' I said. 'I'll handle that one when it comes.'

The chief executive chomped his way through a great mound of bacon and sausages while the rest, stunted by conscience, made do with bagels and cream cheese.

The plan was that during the day I would occupy a bungalow owned by the studio on a street on the other side of Coldwater Canyon, to write the American pilot of *Butterflies* with a man named Joseph Miltonberg. His task was to guide me towards the American language. I was to be picked up each morning at eight o'clock by my baby driver and returned to my hotel at six. Apart from a driver, we had at our disposal a secretary and a 'runner', who literally ran around after us. He parked the car, fetched lunch, made coffee, put flowers on the desk, pulled the blinds down, pointed the cooling fans in the right direction – and supplied endless gags in the hope that he would get one of them into the script, for which he would want an 'additional material by' credit and a large fee.

As the first day unfolded, I could feel the nightmare gathering speed. There were no quiet moments, no time to think things out. Joseph sat opposite me with my original script in front of him. I was supposed to change each line into his spoken version, and the regurgitated script came fast and furious. The runner darted about the room uttering jokes of the lowest level; these were corrected by Joseph, who spoke the terrible results out to me who had to write them down. As soon as I reached the final sentence on a page, the runner would whip the page away and hand it to the neurotic typist who sat three yards away. She would bash it out and then sit with fingers poised waiting for the next creative rendering. Each time I winced, Joseph would triumphantly remind me that he had written for Jack Benny for forty years and the typist and the runner would say, in monotonous unison, 'Yeh – isn't that really something?'

That night, I crawled into my king-size bed and rang my entire family. I needed to hear things which I knew and understood. I had come to dread the words dollar, deal, gag, pitch, hi and Beatle Land. I hated the blue skies, the perfect palms and the effortless ability everyone had to be brown and thin.

Three weeks later, the script was finished. There had been fifteen deliveries to the studio and fourteen rejections. I had lost as many pounds in weight, except that on everyone else it looked good. I was so mentally tired that I had to feel my way into the limousine every morning, and the runner had the new task of hauling me out again at the other end. The smiling American noticed that I was slowly diminishing. He invited me to stay at his and his wife's mountain home. I spent two days alone in their bungalow trying to ward off the coyotes. At night the owners would come home, and we would have dinner and endless discussions about who we should cast for the lead in *Butterflies*. With a heartfelt cry I requested to go home and return for the making of the show.

'Why do you want to go home – is there something we can do?'

'I miss my dog.'

'You want a dog! We'll get you a dog.'

'I want my own dog.'

'Look, honey, if you stay here and come up with the series, you could wind up with a house on Third Street and ten dogs. You could sit by your pool writing scripts. You could have a secretary, a runner. That limousine out there could be yours, honey – you got that? *Yours*.'

I left a note at the hotel desk. It read: 'See you in studio – thanks for everything. Love, Carla.'

The driver, whose ambition now was to play one of the sons in *Butterflies*, sped me to the airport.

'When I get back,' he said, 'I'll read your script. See what I can do with it.'

'Oh, fine,' I said. 'When you've finished pass it to the doorman.'

He smiled a hundred-thousand-dollar cosmetic-dentistry smile. 'Sure,' he said. 'He's a good rewriter – one of the best.'

Rehearsals of the final series of *Bread* had already begun in London. It was a case of straight from the airport to Acton. I had to think about a new series. This is always a very pressurizing time. My mind was overcrowded with anxiety, mostly to do with the horrendous script I had churned out in America, but there was still the need to leave my house in Holland Park. The tiny garden could no longer house my ever-growing assortment of animals. I had put the house up for sale before I left and now there seemed to be a potential buyer.

Frantically – amidst everything else – I began to search for another place to live and then *he* sent a note with a picture of Zoffany House, which was situated on the riverside in Chiswick. The note said, 'This looks like your kind of thing,' so I hurtled off to see it. Zoffany House was a Queen Anne building. The German painter, Johann Zoffany (1733–1810), had lived the last ten years of his life in it. It was for me passion on sight. As soon as I stepped from the rather mundane road at the back, through the large gates and into the long paved garden it had to be mine. Inside was derelict.

Nobody had lived there for over a year, but I could see images of how it could be as I wandered through the arched hall out to the tall windows so close to the water. 'I'll have it,' I said, and I rushed home to phone the bank.'

Ruby Wax bought my house. She came in like a whirlwind and, although her American accent reminded me of the dread of going back to Los Angeles, her obvious talent for amusing dialogue and observations warmed me to her.

'I know about you,' she said. 'You're kind of nuts about animals and things, aren't you?'

'I am, yes.'

'Well, hell, why not? There's room for all of us. The only difference we have is that if you see a tree, you say, "Oh look, a tree!", whereas I say, "Oh look, wood!"' She gave me a little push. 'So let's have a look at this place, OK?'

With another trip to Los Angeles looming up, it was decided that my sister Marna and her husband Leonard would move into Zoffany House with me. There they would have a self-contained flat. I liked the idea of having 'family' in charge, and Marna was, and still is, truly in charge – unlike me, who cannot face domesticity. She has picked up her magic wand and wafted it around whatever house we have ended up in. Her gentle bullying terrorizes even the dust, and when she clangs that big brass bell in the kitchen the parrots are silenced, the cats leap in through the windows and crouch on their marks and any human within its sound stands to immediate attention.

I was summoned to America just before the moving process. A dear friend named Harry Davies lent me his flat in which to house my animals in the interim, and my brother-in-law Leonard moved in to look after them while I was away. With *Bread* coming to an end I had started to write *Screaming* now. The BBC deadline was closing in on me and I had to go in to rehearsals of *Bread* on the day of departure to shorten the script, which was four minutes too long. When I got there I was greeted by dear Jean Boht, who was clasping a tiny bird to her.

'I found this baby duck,' she said. 'I kept putting it back in the pond, but it sank.'

I took the bedraggled bird from her. 'The reason it kept sinking,' I said, 'is because it's a pigeon, not a duck.'

During rehearsals I sat with the yellow bundle on my lap. I had been up to the restaurant for some rice and I fed it while they rehearsed the amended script. Although there was much laughter on the floor about Jean and her 'duck', I sensed a big black cloud hanging over everything. In order to cut the script I had eliminated a short filming sequence. The very talented – and very emotional – actor whose scene it was was now spitting out his lines with venom. The producer, knowing very well why he was doing this, chose to ignore it, hoping he would regain his normal charming disposition, but the whole scene deteriorated into a monosyllabic drone as the contagious discontent spread throughout the cast.

The producer suddenly threw up his hands. 'Oh, come on! What have we got here – a funeral?'

The deprived actor sat down and dropped his head into his hands. I went to him. 'I'm sorry, it was essential. Cutting little bits would not have solved the problem. We were looking for four minutes.'

He was silent. They were all silent.

'You have got quite a lot in this episode,' ventured the producer.

Even more silent silence.

'I have to go to the airport now,' I said.

The actor stood up, punched the table and then sent a harmless kick towards the chair. I left just as he was about to demolish the rest of the props. I phoned home from reception.

'I'm sending a baby pigeon – can you cope?' I asked Leonard.

'One of your other pigeons has escaped,' he said.

'Which one?'

'Bell.'

'Oh, God, not Bell.'

'Don't worry, I'll find him.'

I went to the airport with *him* with turmoil in my stomach. The script of *Screaming* was late and the rehearsal rooms were beset with problems. I hated where I was going. I hadn't had time to check the plumbers and the electricians in Zoffany House – and now Bell was loose, Bell the human bird, Bell who trusted everybody's shoulder, Bell who would land on the head of an unsuspecting passer-by and peer downwards into their face to receive a kiss! Somewhere in the shambles of my departure he said something like, 'There really isn't room in your life for anyone else, is there?' My reply was to dash to the phone and ring Leonard.

'Any sign of Bell?'

'He's sitting in the oak tree in the garden.' I went back and told *him*.

'Oh, great,' he said flatly, and this time there was no exchange of little plastic cards. When I arrived in Los Angeles there was a message: Bell had literally pecked his way into the aviary.

The show was awful. Nothing like *Butterflies*. I didn't recognize any of it. The subtle relationship between Ria and Leonard which I had taken several episodes to build had been crammed into one pilot. All the dollars in the universe would not have compensated for my disappointment. The American producer, a dark, bearded man with a bright yellow cap who carried a rolled multi-coloured umbrella around with him, walked like a god amongst the ecstatic audience. The cast bowed so often that I thought they might snap at the hip.

At the end of the whole thing, we went to yet another luxurious restaurant, where a party had been arranged for my departure. They sat me next to a big tank with three lobsters in it.

'I can't eat here,' I said.

'Why? What's wrong?'

'I can't eat in a place where lobsters are being boiled alive.'

'Oh, come on, honey, this is your night. You're a hit.'

'Thank you, but no.'

The harassed producer, who had been heard describing me as the 'Mad English Lady', asked the manager to cover the tank.

But I had a better idea. As I made what I hoped would be my last getaway from Los Angeles, I thanked the driver for taking the lobsters down to the coast, which was less than a mile away.

'No problem. How much did they cost, by the way?'

'I don't know,' I said. 'I put them on the producer's bill.'

I had come to like my driver. He wore all the hallmarks of the 'I want to be a star' brigade, but without doubt those muscles and the Jesus Christ face would one day reach their goal. When I see American shows on British television, I am always looking out for him.

Chapter 9

My arrival at Zoffany House resembled the moving in of a circus. Horrified neighbours watched the unloading of three dogs, five cats, five hundred assorted birds, six lame, flightless or brain-damaged pigeons, four rabbits, two guinea pigs, a box of assorted fledglings, two tortoises and Bell, who sat on my head whilst I grovelled about in the van for an escaped rabbit.

Later, when everything slept, I inspected my new home. The sun was setting and the deep red river threw scarlet light on to the ceiling; the black silhouette of a pair of Canada geese drifted through the darkness. In the early morning, full of excitement, I wandered around the garden. The sun was rising behind the cottages across the river. Clouds of insects gathered at the tree tops. The mallard ducks preened and bathed on the island bank, and a lone cormorant made a final bid to catch an unsuspecting fish. He threw himself off the mast of a large boat and amidst a great spray of water, he gathered up the fish and took it off to a safe eating place. I could see it wriggling as he flew, its silver belly flashing – and suddenly I was beset by the same harrowing thoughts which always visit me when something comes to its end. The feeling of 'why?'. *Why* this unjust reward to one already engaged in an endless struggle? I console myself with the thought that perhaps the fish, like those who have died, is going on to an Elysian ocean and that the triumphant predator, like those of us still living, is in fact the poorer of the two.

One of my frailties is that I am an extremist. I can never run half a race – or even one race – I have to run two. This was evident during the Zoffany House days. I read about the paramyxo virus which affects birds, mostly pigeons. It vandalizes the nervous system, rendering the bird incapable of eating and finally of flying. The oak tree in my garden was already garnished with feral pigeons who came to feast on the scatterings for my rescued ones, and as I watched through the window one day I recognized the symptoms in a young ginger-coloured bird. During the next three days, in between trying to catch him, I studied the paramyxo virus fiercely. By the time the pigeon was in my net I was the leading world expert. After a couple of days of care and hand feeding, I took the bird down to my friends Peter and Karen, who were running a sanctuary in Dorset – and who were the second leading experts. Only hours later, I spotted two more, their heads twisting, their feathers fluffed, deep in the grip of this ruthless virus. The sickness was spreading rapidly in London and the pigeons caught on that I was running an intensive-care unit. Within one week I had taken in twenty-five more birds and I was spending my days hanging by my boots from the oak tree, dropping the sadly ruffled creatures into a basket and charging down to Dorset.

Now I was obsessed. Everywhere I went, my practised eye scanned the various flocks settled in the parks or in the trees, or simply minding their own business on the pavements or in shop doorways. Every now and then my eager antennae would pick up a weak one, and with a cry of 'sick bird!' I would grind to a halt, hold up the traffic and hurl myself on to the unsuspecting patient before he could get his stricken body into the take-off position. People raised their eyes to heaven and pointed to their heads, indicating my madness. Someone reported me to the police, saying that there was a strange-looking blonde taking pigeons off the streets for vivisection and down in Dorset they were frantically building a fifty-foot aviary to house them. What, you may ask, was it all for? Vets had been instructed to destroy the virused pigeons. It took over a year to nurse each bird back to full health. A year of hand feeding and constant watch – but then comes the moment when the mended bird, not in the least grateful, beating you impatiently with his wings, desperate to get to the sky, suddenly takes his first flight and makes his first wobbly landing. There is a pause while he tries to remember how he was and, finally, off he goes on a strong and steady journey. The real reward comes later when all of them, in a great coloured cloud, encircle the place where they were nursed. Not just once, but three times a day. And this mystical recognition goes on until the end of their life.

With my new script delivered, I was getting ready to go to a meeting at the BBC Television Centre. The Head of Comedy wanted to see me. Marna threw the mail on to my bed and reminded me that I was late. I caught sight of a rather rich cream-coloured envelope. It bore a royal crest. I opened it – and my eyes picked out words like 'Her Majesty', 'the Prime Minister', 'OBE'. I couldn't quite grasp it – an OBE. *Me?* What for? It's a joke, someone is winding me up. I read it again. I held it up to the light. I turned it upside down. I wanted to go and tell Marna, ring my mother, my sons, my friends, but there was this thing about secrecy. Marna put her head around the door.

'Anything to shout about?'

'No,' I said, 'bills as usual.'

I hid the envelope in a drawer amongst my knickers and I left the house with the idea that if it was still there when I came home it was real.

The Head of Comedy came from behind his desk and sat in the chair next to me. He was the same charming coffee-offering person who usually occupies that particular office, and after asking me how I was, and the new house and all the animals, he looked at me gravely. 'It's about your writing.'

My heart somersaulted.

'It's – it's . . .' He searched desperately for a suitably undamaging remark. 'It's lost its sense of fun.'

My mind wandered to the drawer in my bedroom, and the contents gave me a momentary flow of confidence. 'If you mean I don't write gags, you're right. I don't like gags. I try to write dialogue. I try to be real.' A fountain of defence had sprung up now. 'Comedy should be about people and life and emotions. I can't write the yuk-yuk stuff that you seem to want.'

He looked at me for a long time, long enough for me to realize that I had just made the most arrogant speech – one which would not endear the man to me at all.

'You are working for the media, Carla. The media is working for the public. To a degree, we must give them what they want, and in your case they want to laugh. That is why you are a comedy writer and not a drama writer. That is what you are paid to do.'

'But *Bread* is way up there in the ratings,' I said.

'Yes, but this script' – he patted it – 'this script is

going back to the days before *Bread* – the days of *Leaving* and *I Woke Up One Morning*. Oh, beautifully written, but not *funny*, Carla.'

I was mixed up. I had liked *Leaving*, I had loved *I Woke Up One Morning*, but the viewers had not responded – the ratings were not good. I fell into a deep melancholia. Somehow I had come complete circle. There was the beginning when I was totally unimportant, when actors and actresses changed my lines, when during the filming, on cold, wet days, the producer and the entire crew would rush to cover the stars with an umbrella while I stood there with my bra filling up with rain. If I saw something in rehearsals that I did not approve of, my voice came out in a tiny squeak – and even that was frozen into silence by mass staring. After the script no one wanted me. I was patted on the head and sent back to Liverpool. Then the glimpse of success: interviews, articles, the phone ringing, photographs. The slow moving to the hierarchy of top programme – more press, more photographs. If I sneezed it went into print. There were invitations to open things, attend things, give lectures, be honorary this and honorary that. Finally, after eighteen years of this, the teacher had called me in and taken away my gold star.

Back home now, I opened the drawer. It was still there. 'Her contributions to the arts' it said, and the thought plagued my mind that by the time I went to receive it, I would be a failure.

The following night was studio night, which is a mixture of emotions. Even if the show has gone well during the week in rehearsals, you can never be sure on the night of recording it. Sometimes actors who have given you a perfect rendering all week suddenly grow tired of their own presentation and give you something different in the studio. This new offering can be better or worse – or disastrous, which is why the theory that we are only as good as the last thing we did becomes terrifying. The gallery is the engine room of it all. There sits the producer, his assistant, the vision mixer, the resource coordinator, the gallery visitors and myself. The rooms on either side house the lighting and the grams – meaning sound. The producer is in contact with the floor manager, who wears earphones and works with the cast on the floor, and messages of approval or hysteria are relayed from one to the other. An important factor here is, of course, the audience – a much-feared beast – for their reaction, be it accurate or not, dictates the success of the show. Often a scene which seemed hilarious in rehearsal fails to bring that hoped-for noise, whereas a scene which we had not thought particularly funny sends them into a writhing mass. This unpredictability is the essence of excitement, the adventure, the reason for enduring the solitude and the stress which precedes it. A show played well brings pride, and revitalizes a battered confidence; a disappointing reaction to a show brings catatonic depression and thoughts of suicide.

This particular night was a night of survival. In a series that has been running for a while and in which the characters have become well-loved there is a kind of unison amongst the audience. Fluffs and mistakes are not important and when pans fall off the shelves because an actress slams a door none of it matters and it adds to the general fun. Often we actually had to plead with the audience not to laugh too much and drown the actors' lines. On the last night there is always a party, with its hugs and kisses and presents, with its praise and gratitude ringing out. And after that, each one went off into the sunset, some to return for more accolades, others never to be seen again.

I was becoming radical, militant even, about the welfare of animals. People were beginning to hear that I rescued pigeons, and consequently I was receiving letters with tales of horror, tales of shooting, poisoning, snaring and of a general cruel attitude towards these intelligent and intriguing birds.

One morning, stuck in a traffic jam, I noticed a huge net stretched beneath a bridge. When I looked carefully,

I could see a couple of pigeons struggling to get free from it. As soon as I could I phoned the appropriate council. They were evasive. At first they denied putting it there. Finally, after at least six different calls, I spoke to someone of authority who admitted that it was a 'deterrent'. I explained that it was the breeding season and that young birds trapped in nests behind the nets would starve, not to mention the frantic parents getting caught in an attempt to go to their young. He promised to have it removed immediately, and he kept his word. I suppose the incident gave me the idea that I could use my name to help the cause which haunted me, and from that realization came 'Animaline', a non-profit-making company set up by myself to be a voice for the animals. Now I was being referred to as a crank. At first it angered me, but one day I was having lunch with a very famous actress. She looked at me and patted my hand. 'Carla, darling, we know you're a crank but we still love you.' She picked up a little roasted quail from her plate and tore it apart, then swallowed it with relish. I remember thinking, Long may we reign.

The White-Coated Man

(Song about Vivisection)

Sometime today he will set me free.
I will hear a voice and it will be
The white-coated man.
Where are the leaves – what happened – why this
    pain?
Sometime today he will set me free,
And again I will hear a voice and it will be
The white-coated man.

Chorus:

If man wants life and eternity,
Then man must pay and man must see
That we are theirs to mind,
For man is the word, man is the law,
If man gets sick, he will find a cure.
The white-coated man.

Somewhere out there I can hear them laughing.
Do they know about me, why can't I see?

Chorus:

And they will pay, the silent ones will pay,
The silent ones will pay.

The first really important step towards speaking for the animals came when I wrote to Mr Gummer, the Minister for Agriculture, and requested an appointment. He quickly replied and I visited his office in London. My plea then was for the animals which were being transported live to other countries for slaughter. I pointed out that apart from the journey and the constant fear, there was the eventual arrival at slaughterhouses which were places of untold horror.

Mr Gummer sat on the edge of his chair. He was obviously in a hurry, so were the other two gentlemen who were with him. However, he listened to me patiently and then, in his best minister's voice, he said, 'Of course, Miss Lane, you may not be aware of the fact that animals going abroad are only sent to selected abattoirs and we, the government, have gone a long way towards bringing these places up to scratch – especially in Spain.'

I could not believe that the man in charge of our animal welfare should actually believe that a modernized slaughterhouse would be of any benefit to the animals concerned. I recalled how once a government spokesman on the subject of vivisection defended the scientists who were torturing their helpless charges, by rejoicing in the aseptic condition of the laboratories – the criteria being in both cases that you can 'beat the dog to death as long as his kennel is clean'.

I asked the minister if he had brought the *Spaniards* up to scratch. He looked at me in a puzzled way, then suddenly his face lit up. He had thought of a suitable retort. 'Well, come now, you don't expect us to change a whole nation, do you?'

I wanted to say, 'No, Mr Gummer, I do not, but you *are*. You are changing us, the British. You are putting live creatures in the hands of people who by their nature do not care – and you are doing this very un-English thing for no other reason than the French bellies!' But somehow I felt that these dark-suited men, sitting in their dark brown office, had no conception of the cruelty involved. Their large cars, the sense of their own importance, their comfortable existence, left no room for reality. They, as politicians, must go where money reigns. What has a sheep giving birth just before going for slaughter or a cow travelling to its death for a day and a night without food or water got to do with them? Their mission is to promote the growth of our new world in the hope that the bully boys with their electric probes, the self-seeking scientists who harm and vandal-ize living, feeling creatures, the factory farmers, the exporters, the profit-making abusers will be lost or go unnoticed in its materialistic splendour.

I left the building feeling despair. The press had found out that I was visiting, and they crowded the entrance. Mr Gummer arranged for me to be smuggled out the back way. As I drove home, I thought about how the human race disappoints me. Our gastronomic greed and financial fanaticism masks much of our excellence. The terrible plight of all creatures is that we are in charge of the planet, science is moving too fast, we are losing sight of the acceptable and whilst governments sit making distant rules the universe is suffocating. Man himself has changed – he is no longer safe from his own kind. Perhaps just before we shrivel the earth completely we will live to see the most terrifying thing of all, the end product of genetic engineering: man-made man.

A part of the writer's derangement is the fascination of the human animal – the greatness of it and the tyranny. We are made up of as many bad things as good and this distinguishes us from other animals, which on the whole have a larger percentage of good. They are not gifted with reasoning and so everything is done with sincere intent, like the lion chasing the zebra for no other reason than that he is hungry. Not so the human. We endure a knowledge of outcome, but still we commit mental and physical atrocities on our kind as well as on the rest. Even when in love, that feverish state of blissful blob, we hurl harsh words and plot unseen traps for our loved one in an effort to stay part of the strenuous game of life and intrigue.

Really Nice Lover: 'I don't mind if you feel the need

to sleep with someone else, so long as you tell me. All I want is the truth, then I can walk away.'

Really Nice Truthful Lover: 'Well, I wasn't going to tell you this, but whilst you were away I did. But it didn't mean anything – it's you I love.'

Really Nice Lover Turning Nasty: 'It doesn't matter. All I needed you to do was tell me. See if I care. You were never very good at it anyway.'

Cow
(Song)

Placid creature,
Standing in your June field,
With one more day of grazing
Before the slatted truck.

And when it comes
You will go – with quiet dignity,
Across the yard, up the ramp,
Into the dark.

And as you meet
The final man,
There will be nothing on your face
Save the familiar beauty.
And he will eat you,
Because he didn't look.

Chapter 10

My sons came to London to go with me to receive my OBE. We took my well-loved but seldom used Mercedes, and we cruised to the Palace. I was aware that this was a once-in-a-lifetime event, and I soaked each moment in. At the entrance to the Palace itself, I had to take a different route and leave Carl and Nigel. I walked along the huge hallway, with its deep red carpets and rare paintings. I stopped in front of a portrait by Zoffany. My mind was saying, I live in your house now, Zoff (which was my pet name for him). I've sat on your tombstone eating chocolate cake served by the Chiswick Church, and now I've stood before your work. Which room did you die in, Zoff?

Passing the alcoves with the handsomely dressed guardsmen standing there like porcelain soldiers, perfectly poised, no trace of movement or any expression on their faces, I came to a large hall where other recipients had gathered. A gentleman in a dark uniform embellished with gold braid was putting us into groups, after which he instructed us how to present ourselves to the Queen. Four paces forward, turn to face her, two paces forward, receive honour, two paces back, curtsy and leave. I was besieged with panic. I had never walked backwards before, and I was wearing high heels. I could see the tabloid headlines: 'Scriptwriter takes a tumble in the Palace', or 'Ceremony held up as Carla crashes in Palace'.

My heart was beating as I lined up, and the sight of the huge audience and the band playing softly in the gallery sent a wave of terror through me.

'You write, don't you?'

The Queen, small and with that wide, sudden smile, stood on a scarlet platform. She was wearing a pale yellow silk suit. It was quite creased. I remember thinking how 'normal' it made her look.

'I try, Your Majesty,' I replied modestly.

She pinned the medal on my lapel. 'Keep it up, well done,' she said.

I stepped back, curtsied, turned right and away. I was so relieved that I completely lost my bearings. I headed for the nearest exit and followed a corridor. Then, to my dismay, I found myself gliding across the stage again – past the Queen, past the audience and out through the arch which I should have gone through in the first place. There was no sound from the audience, no look of concern from the Queen. Everybody simply accepted that I was an idiot lost, and the gentleman about to receive his OBE waited generously whilst I made this involuntary lap of honour.

In the courtyard we posed for photographs. The professionals were there, gently bullying us into holding our medals up and adjusting our posture. The sun shone on the cobbles and the yard rang with shrill ladies' voices and men's protests as they were urged to pose with their top hat tucked beneath their arm and their white gloves in one hand resting nonchalantly across the other. My black and beautiful Mercedes still wears the green Palace car park sign. Nobody can tell what it is. It serves to remind me, in periods of diminishing self-esteem, that not all my time has been wasted.

After three years in Zoffany House I met Michael Winner. He rang my agent and we met for lunch. He is a large, loud man and he has no problems with talking straight. After knowing him for a while, you begin to cherish his truthfulness and his ability to see things just as they are and not as you would like them to be. His idea was that we should become partners in a production company. I explained that I was just beginning to write another series for the BBC which would take me almost a year. 'I'll wait, darling,' he said, and during that year we occasionally met – once in his house for lunch. It is a beautiful place. We sat at the end of a magnificent table. His cook, a shy Scottish lady, put as much effort and thought into our meal as if she were catering for a big party. And afterwards, as he went down the stairs, Michael suddenly disappeared into a huge cupboard. I could hear his muffled voice as he sifted his way though various stored paintings. 'I'll give you a picture of consequence, darling,' he said and he emerged with a lovely, decorative Victorian drawing with notes by the artist on the back. It was framed in black and gold and as he handed it to me he said, 'There, take it – and be quiet.'

Before the year was up, the BBC had heard about my plan to join Michael. I suppose this was the reason they suddenly trebled my money and offered me a contract for three years. I was dumbfounded. I rang my agent, who advised me to take it as I had already expressed fear about the business side of a production company. I am not equipped to be involved or to handle such things, so I wrote to Michael and explained. 'Take it, darling,' he said. 'It's about time they realized what you're fucking worth.'

We have been good friends since. In the days when Jenny Seagrove lived with him she often called me as she had fallen into the habit of rescuing sick pigeons. She would sit in the kitchen gently offering baby food to the young bird, her old dog, Sacha, applauding her with adoring and attentive eyes. The large and somewhat confused Michael fidgeted and paced about.

'It fell out of its bloody nest, darling,' he said, almost accusingly. He pulled a chair out and pushed it back in again. He didn't look at the bird. 'God knows which nest it was. There are dozens of the bloody things out there.' The words came out sharply, almost angrily, but somewhere in the man you could sense a great compassion.

My contract brought me a whole new wealth. No more the writing on spec, no more the waiting for repeat money. Everything was put together and four times a year I received an enviable sum of money. This was lethal for my already money-unconscious attitude and within weeks I was hurling it about as if it were confetti. I bought three of everything, the maxim being one for me, one for my mother and another in case anybody else wanted one. I lavished surprises on my family, had an enormous unit with heated cabins built for my rescued birds, catapulted to Rome, Paris, Venice. Took my mother, my daughters-in-law and anybody else who happened to be around when I was making the booking. Bought bicycles for little boys who stood outside shops with noses flattened against the windows, sent cheques to animal sanctuaries and generally crowded my life with self-indulgent bits and pieces. By the time the second contract was received I had become irresponsible, believing that as long as I got my scripts in on time I could call upon the monetary reservoir whenever I needed. I was still writing *Screaming*, and my head was spurting out ideas like a Roman candle. I had a secretary to attend to my mail, and not *one* cleaning lady, but three. Soon I had garaged my Merc and was hurtling around in a new Range Rover with a Vodaphone hanging from my ear and the elegant Maximus lounging on the back seat. All I needed to complete this madness was a helicopter overhead playing the title music from *Dallas*.

And then something happened to put an end to it all. I was in the bathroom when Maximus came into the room and rested his noble head on the edge of the bath. It was a strange thing for him to do. He seemed distressed. I put on my bathrobe and took him into the garden. He just sat staring at me. 'What is it, Maximus? What's wrong?' I was filled with dread. Something awful was happening. He lay down quietly – his eyes could not stay open. I phoned the locum vet. 'My dog is ill.'

'Take him to your own vet tomorrow morning.'

'He needs to be seen now.'

'You'll have to bring him in.'

'But you're a long way from here, and he is too ill.'

'Sorry, we can't come out.'

I put the phone down. Maximus had climbed on to my bed – a thing he never did – and was trying to dig a hole in it. His mouth was wide open and he couldn't breathe. I frantically phoned again. The vet's wife answered.

'My dog is desperately ill. Can your husband come out?'

'My husband can't leave the surgery in case an emergency comes in.'

'But this is an emergency.'

'Can't you bring him in?'

'He weighs thirteen stone, and he can't walk.'

'Then put him on a blanket and drag him to the car.'

I couldn't believe what I was hearing. I slammed the phone down and went to Maximus. He looked glazed and weary. I put his collar on. 'Come on, my sweetheart, just make it to the car, will you?' His great body drew itself up and he followed me bravely and steadily to the car. I helped him on to the seat. An hour later I was still trying to find the surgery, which was situated in a quiet road amidst a one-way traffic system. As soon as I got out of the car, Maximus once again gathered his strength and followed me along the drive and into the surgery where the vet was waiting. When he saw the man in the white coat, it was if he understood that here was help so he could rest. He collapsed on the floor, legs spread-eagled. The man was slow and imprecise. He gave Maximus an injection and it was obvious that he didn't know what was wrong. 'It's no good me keeping him in,' he said. 'There's no one here to take care of him if I'm called out.' It was two o'clock in the morning. 'I suggest you take him home and see how he is in the morning.'

'What is it? What is it?' I asked.

'I don't know,' he replied.

'Can you help me to lift him?' The man looked at me astounded. 'He's a big dog,' he said. I felt desperate and defeated. I knelt down in front of Maximus and touched his closed eyes. 'Come on, sweetheart, one more time.'

Maximus walked beside me as if nothing was wrong. His beautiful head hung low, but his body moved with the usual stealth and grace. I opened the car door and placed his two front paws on the seat, and as I began to lift him in he grew embarrassed and struggled on to the seat without my help. 'Good boy,' I said, and I reached to stroke his face. He was dead.

I parked the car outside Zoffany House and I sat there until first light. My chest ached with grief and I kept turning to look at him in case I was wrong. He did not look dead. His eyes were bright and healthy, his face had a devilish look about it, as if he was about to tantalize me with an enormous paw. The birds had begun to sing now and I could hear my pigeons cooing on the other side of the wall. I took off Maximus's collar and gently stroked his head, then I covered him with his blanket and I went into the house.

It was an empty, cold place. I mechanically fed the cats and the birds, then I phoned my friend Dr Dick White, who practises at the Veterinary College in Cambridge. I babbled incoherently. 'I'll come right away,' he said. At one o'clock I delivered Maximus's body to a place in Paddington.

That night, when it was dark, I took the car and searched for a skip. Maximus's bed was still on the back seat, and it was heavily stained with blood. I found a skip in a quiet road in Notting Hill Gate. I tossed his bed and his blankets into it, then I sat in the car and I knew exactly where the words 'heartache' came from.

Remember Maximus

There are moments when the umbrella of sorrow
    hangs over me.
I question the chaffinch's song,
And there seems to be no reason for the
    buttercups.

It was rehearsals the next day. I got there early so I could bathe my puffed-up eyes with cold water, and I sat alone in the huge rehearsal room waiting for the cast to arrive. Dick had phoned me. Maximus had died from 'torsion', which means a twisted gut. It probably happened while he was running in the park, and it is common among big dogs. 'He couldn't have been saved,' said Dick. 'But the pain could have been alleviated if he had been attended to sooner.' It was then that I realized how wasteful my life had become. Without explanation my mind was busy recycling my priorities. It was forcing me to ask and to answer uncomfortable questions about myself, and by the time the first actress arrived I had decided that money was fine if it was used properly. Big cars are fine providing you don't mind them getting dirty, jewellery is fine providing you don't have to have a bodyguard whilst you're wearing it. One cleaner is enough, and secretaries are pretentious. My brain was telling me, I suppose, that it was Maximus who had enriched my life.

'Carla, darling.'

The cast came towards me. We rehearsed, we laughed, we had lunch and I drove home.

I was pleased with *Screaming*. Watching fine actresses put life into my words was always an uplifting experience. Because the dialogue was rather tense at times, it was suggested that we ask the BBC to let us record it without an audience. Penny Wilton had said, 'I find it difficult to deliver my lines – some of which are a little profound – knowing that it will be greeted with a mechanical titter.' We made our worries known, but the BBC felt that 'comedy should have the benefit of audience reaction'. There was a degree of unrest among us. Penny must have felt 'unlistened to', but there was no visible problem.

Screaming was aired and got the usual caustic treatment, but I was feeling calm, almost tranquil. Now that my secretary and two of the cleaners had gone, the house was less crowded. I began to save money. By the end of the series I was driving round in a mud-spattered Range Rover, and I had returned to the sanity of my northern roots. We had the usual end-of-programme party, and raised our glasses to the next series without too much incident. Life was being kind all round. My family was safe and prospering. My mother was still charging round in her high heels and, as she would put it, 'Running rings round the young ones.'

But because of my natural fear of too many good times, and the question always being 'Where is the rub?', I was always thoughtful when I was being lucky and sometimes, when I was driving through London with my favourite opera playing and a well-loved dog in the back, I found myself thinking a prayer. It always went something like, 'Please look after those who are in peril, bless the animals and keep my family safe.' I was never quite sure who I was praying to – God or Nature itself. But even as I pleaded, bad times were crouching in a distant crevice.

During my previous spending days, my sons had told me about an island off the coast of Wales. The deer had all died on it because there was no food left there. It was for sale and I uttered the usual phrase – 'Buy it.' Two months later it was mine, and now I was longing to see this place which I had bought so casually.

On a bright June day, I set off in a helicopter provided by a newspaper. I prepared myself to behold a rather grim-looking rock, which I decided to think of as a giant birdcage. My first glimpse of St Tudwal's East was as we crossed the mainland at Abersoch; a curious green and brown lump rising out of the sea. Mildly impressed, I transferred to the boat I had equally so casually bought and at six o'clock in the evening, with the sun playing deep gold tricks with the sea, I climbed up the rocks and on to the plateau. There in a warm hollow just beside the little croft a young hind was giving birth. She had obviously been the only survivor of this tragic island. Dotted about were the skeletons of dead deer but close to the hind lay the body of her stag, with its fine head propped up on a small stone. His was the only carcass that had remained in full fur, perhaps nature had arranged this to give her comfort during her lonely pregnancy.

The new baby deer made noisy news on the mainland.

We had left the island immediately to give her privacy, and by nine o'clock that same evening we were sitting in the local pub watching a newsflash on the television heralding this arrival.

When I returned to the island, I was immediately struck by it. The clear waters held shadows of dolphins and seals. The slopes were covered with wild flowers, small black rabbits amongst them, ears and heads popped up from clumps of fern and tall green grass. A lizard streaked up the wall of the croft, frogs sat on the edge of a spring, a herd of Soya sheep stood looking quizzically down at us from an overhanging bank, and at the top of the plateau gutsy seabirds of every kind came out of the air and brushed our heads, their cries warning us to keep away from their nests. The ground was littered with little clusters of grey chicks, some neatly deposited in discarded rabbit holes, and to complete nature's tapestry the young hind carefully came out from a cave in the rocks. She raised her head and tested the air and, as if she had signalled 'no danger', the three-day-old fawn joined her. There was no sign of weakness or nerves. Already he was steady on his legs and they stood close together looking like a painting on a porcelain plate.

The sight of these things made me decide that this blob of earth was never to be invaded by man, but would remain a place of dignity and safety for all time. I

The Island

My untainted bit of the planet.

1   Entrance to the lovely old croft on the island. It was
    built in the twelfth century. The monks used it for
    prayers and there are three tombs beneath its floor.
    These cannot be disturbed because the floor is solid,
    and damage would be irreparable.

2   Carl, Nigel and me making our way to the island –
    I fell out of the boat a few moments after this was
    taken!

3   The natural spring on the island. This makes it
    possible for the animals to survive. Carl and Nigel
    look after it and keep it pure. When I first bought
    the island, the spring was full of dead deer.

4   The ridge on the island of St Tuwal's East. Its twin
    island, St Tuwal's West, is in the background.

5   Me. The notice, which is written in English and
    Welsh, requests that people do not trespass and that
    they leave the island to nature and its resident
    creatures.

ordered two notices to be made – one in English, one in Welsh – politely reminding people that St Tudwal's had been handed over to nature.

I had written four more scripts when the BBC told me that one of the stars no longer wished to play the part. This plunged me into an unsurmountable situation. I knew it would be fatal to recast her – she was so right in the part, and the series was too new to start replacing main characters. On the other hand, the four scripts had taken me ten weeks to write, and if I started something new I wouldn't have time to fulfil my contract of fifteen scripts a year. Total panic set in. I lay awake at night trying to rid my mind of the characters I had so carefully built and replace them with totally different ones. While I tried to call upon new names and new faces, the old ones crowded my head. For the first time I had come face to face with the most dreaded of all dreaded things – writer's block. For days I plodded round Chiswick Park, but everywhere I went reminded me of Maximus so I ended up tearfully recalling our days together. I shifted my neurotic self to the Portobello Market, then to the Tate Gallery. I drove to curious places in and around London, parking my car and eating chocolate-covered peanuts as I searched for something which would bring back my vanished skill. I rang my sons. I rang my brother, I rang my mother, I rang all

my friends in the hope that one of them would say
something to light the dying candle – and then, as I sat
in a traffic jam in Kensington Church Street, I saw him:
a small man wearing an expensive suit and carrying a
briefcase. He was trying to hail a taxi. They were all
occupied, and as he passed in front of my car and gave
my bonnet a frustrated little punch I knew that the
weight of the entire world was strapped to his back.
You probably own a factory, I thought. You probably
have a discontented wife and some horrible kids to
contend with. You're probably having an affair and it's
all too much for you. The man was now embracing a
lady who was carrying a baby. They got into a car
together. He had not been trying to hail a taxi, he had
been trying to get to her on the other side of the road –
a happy family man it now seemed. But too late:
Harold Craven had been born. *Luv* was marching
through my guts begging to be written. Time to pick
up my pen.

I had always been besotted with gypsies. The Romany
way of life held intrigue and mystery for me, and when
I was fifteen I used to tell my father – who in his
seagoing days often visited Spain – 'I want to go to
Granada and join the gypsies there.' I knew that he used
to visit the gypsy caves himself. Indeed, my real name,
which is Romana, was taken from those times, but he
always used to say, 'If you go to the gypsies in Spain,

it's the cockroaches. If you go to them here, it's chipping ice off your boots in the mornings.' So, in a way, I became my own gypsy – always restless, always on the move, always dreaming of forests and flower-spotted fields. Even Zoffany House was losing its hold on me. The river, which sometimes came to my front door, looked dark and lifeless. I was beginning to irritate the neighbours by feeding feral pigeons, which took up permanent residence in the oak tree in my garden, and the field mice which in their hundreds lived in my garage – and sometimes in my car! Also I was witnessing a grave change in the people of London. They were tense, if not aggressive. Even the perfectly correct over-taking process seemed to promote murderous intent and although I loved the buildings and the bustle of a city I could feel the need for good air and open spaces taking over.

Because the property market was at its lowest, I decided to put Zoffany House up for sale. This, I thought, would begin the process of salvaging my rest-lessness, but would also take time, during which I could think and reassess my impatient longing to make this problem-laden move. My theory was that my comple-tion of the first series of *Luv* would obligingly coincide with the sale of my house. I was wrong. Within three weeks Zoffany House had not one but two buyers. I hadn't even finished the first script. Blindly I went ahead, finally promising the house to a charming titled couple who appreciated its history and did not want to massacre it. I had nowhere to go, of course, but brochures were pouring through my letterbox in their hundreds. All I had to do was choose a place and go.

During the following weeks, my brother-in-law, Leonard, drove me over the south of England looking for a place in the wilderness whilst Marna, with her usual ability to take over the house, the animals, the phone calls, the cooking, the general shambles, rescued me from madness. Armed with maps and brochures, we set off each morning, the plan being that he got us there whilst I wrote scripts on the back seat.

Now an even more bizarre plan was fermenting in my mind. I had already committed myself to paying for the upkeep of some horses and birds which belonged to Peter and Karen's sanctuary in Dorset which had now gone bankrupt. Surely the best idea would be to open up my own sanctuary. Peter and Karen could manage it. Yes – brilliant. The road to new triumphs and catastrophes was truly carved. So the amended version was that we were looking for a house with a farm attached, and this made me recall a brochure about Broadhurst Manor. I had put it aside because the house was too big and the complications of running an estate were too much for me, but now it seemed ideal so, on a dark and bitter day, we drove deep into the Sussex countryside. Already

I was questioning my affinity with it. Leaves hung like dead men from the trees, cows and sheep stood motionless with their heads pressed against the great chestnut trunks, previous rain clung to the branches and now and then a stray gust of wind would send it down in an icy shower. The odd tail swished, the odd eye blinked – but that was all. I comforted myself with the thought of spring.

The manor stood in a small valley between the fields. The lane leading to it twisted its way towards a massive iron gate and there, behind an enormous round courtyard, was the house itself. There was a fishpond made of old stone, oak beams, a heavy slated roof, indestructible wooden doors with iron studs and hinges and towering old chimneys. I could hear the clashing of swords and the mixture of steel armoury and horses' hooves on cobblestones. Inside – rich oak panels, fireplaces tall and wide with secret panels in the stone surround, high carved mantelpieces and from every window a breath-stopping view. In spite of the fact that I couldn't really afford it, I heard myself saying, 'I'll take it – it's mine. I can't let anyone else have it.'

The situation now was that in London I had myself, Marna and Leonard waiting to move into the manor, and in Dorset I had Peter and Karen with their six rescued ponies, twenty rescued goats, forty-eight ducks and geese, several hundred sick and disabled pigeons, fifteen cats, eight dogs, a one-winged heron and an assortment of other creatures, all of which had been divested of various bits of their anatomy. My own birds – now six hundred altogether – had to be caught and transported separately, along with my five cats, three dogs, two tortoises, several fish, two rabbits and, of course, Bell, the indestructible pigeon.

The word havoc is not an adequate description of the exodus. On the actual day of the move, Peter and Karen in Dorset were 'packing' their menagerie. The pigeons had to be vaccinated against the paramyxo virus and each animal had to be carefully boxed according to its disability. The one-winged heron, a shy sensitive bird, folded itself intelligently into a seagull size and went without protest into a tea chest. The ponies – still with the New Forest spirit in them – took off across the plains and had to be coaxed back to the horse boxes. The ducks and geese fled to the lake, the hens and cockerels took to the roof and Punk the Polish bantam legged it up the lane towards the motorway.

Meanwhile, back at Zoffany House, the majority of the animals were stacked in their baskets outside, but the birds in the aviary had decided they were not going – so with the removal men stampeding round the house trying to crate the furniture and escape the talons of Daniel, the free-range parrot, I was charging round the conservatory brandishing a net. Finally Peter, with his magic knowledge, had to drive from Dorset to catch the last stubborn batch.

It was dark when the entourage arrived at the manor. Both parties merged at the top of the lane, and the queue of cars, vans, Range Rovers and horse boxes moved steadily towards the stable yard. Each vehicle was manned by a good and true friend, and by torchlight we settled in, fed and watered nearly a thousand animals. There was no panic. The darkness had calmed them all. The horses trotted into the stables as though they had been brought up there, the ducks and geese waddled in behind them and the hens roosted on the horses' backs. The doves left their carriers without stress and flew straight into the rafters of the enclosed barn. The dogs slept in the cottage along with the cats, and the sick pigeons were hand fed and then put in specially prepared and heated units. Somewhere around two o'clock in the morning we sat in a quiet row on the cobbles, too tired to move, too numb to even speak. The gentle cooing of the doves was trailing off, the odd confused chickens were making their final noises as sleep overtook them – and then silence.

Unbeknown to us, in the deserted sanctuary in Dorset one little pigeon huddled in an aviary. He had defied us all and now, with the normally heated cabins derelict, he sat there in the cold, his head twisting and turning as the panic brought back the symptoms of his illness

which in turn created an inability to feed himself. He
need not have worried. At the morning count he was
missed and Peter drove back to Dorset to find him.
Although the bush on which he always roosted had
been overturned, he had perched on its roots and waited.
Not one creature lost.

Goose

She was just a goose
Drifting loose,
Away from the rest,
Because in her chest,
A pellet of lead.

I held her close
As he prepared the dose,
And close to my face,
Resting there,
Her magnificent head.

I could smell her river,
Hear the willows shiver,
See the pulsing sky
Trapped in her eye,
And there she was,
Finished.

Chapter 11

We were having a desperate winter. My sons Carl and Nigel were spending freezing days on my island opening up the spring and taking feed blocks out for the sheep. They built a shelter for them and came back with the news that instead of eight Soya sheep there were now twelve. This meant there was going to be a danger of interbreeding, so I contacted Dr Dick White again to seek his advice.

A week later, on a freezing morning, he, Manda Scott and Richard Eastwood, both brilliant anaesthetists, an assortment of sons and friends and all the gear set off in my small island boat, which crossed the rough waters with the finesse of a road drill.

Soya sheep are very wild. They look like goats and they don't herd like normal sheep, which means that catching them was a major task. Looking through my binoculars from the snug comfort of the hotel lounge, I could see a marked chaos on the island. John Hicks of International Animal Rescue had given me some collapsible fencing. With this a tunnel had been constructed, but the sheep had taken to the rocks and I could see Richard being lowered by his legs with the rest of the crew hanging on to him in an effort to coax them back up on to the plateau.

Well into the evening the boat chugged homewards. It had begun to hail and the wind was ferocious. I worried about the whole idea of the rams being castrated on such a day. I kept imagining what it must have felt like and I noticed as I passed the mirrored door in the hall that I had developed a strangely sympathetic walk.

Dick and his colleagues tumbled into the hotel. They were so cold and wet that Christine, Dick's wife, and I had to hold them up whilst they took their wellies off and guide their immobilized bodies towards selected hot baths.

'All done – all balls off,' muttered Dick as Christine peeled off his frozen green surgeon's gown. Now I could leave my island in the hands of the coming spring and get back to that curious place in which I now lived – Sussex.

Luv was going well. The cast were enjoying it and there were no tantrums on the floor, but I was wrestling with the journey from Sussex to London each morning. To get there for ten thirty I had to leave at seven forty-five.

The tension of the motorway was getting to me. Several times I took wrong turnings and ended up in Sunbury or East Grinstead, but on return the sight of those iron gates at Broadhurst with Igor, the lurcher, acquired in the wake of my grief after losing Maximus, running towards them always gladdened me. It was as if I was entering my own little designer universe: the sound of cockerels and peacocks, ducks on my doorstep, doves, now set free, encircling the land and coming to roost in the barns, fish leaping in the lakes, kingfishers, dragon-flies, woodpeckers – everything stretching and growing, and not a can of insecticide anywhere.

There were, however, underlying hitches. I was learning quickly that when you have land you need not only people to look after it, but equipment – things like tractors, strimmers, lawn cutters, hedge cutters, trailers, wheelbarrows, miles and miles of hosepipes, rakes, spades, hoes. And not just money – but lots of it. The pattern of my life was undergoing a complete metamorphosis. No longer the swishing skirts and velvet tops, it was wellies and waders; no longer the quick jaunt to the shops for forgotten milk (the nearest shop is three miles away), and once hasty lunches with friends had to be arranged days ahead, with the journey to London before and after.

Amidst the immediate tranquillity, I could sense the great tidal wave of worry making its way towards me.

It followed me in the mornings to the sanctuary to feed the sick birds, it hung over me as I helped to drive the rescued ponies up the lane to our field. They gathered in a mischievous bunch and trotted in front of us completely untethered, and I could see their coats glistening, their eyes bright with devilment, their once shrunken bodies hard and strong. And often I wondered whether or not saving this lucky few was contributing anything to the cause as each month thousands more went to the slaughterhouses. My answer always came as I watched them gallop around the paddock: their dignity and poise were equal to their thoroughbred friends in the adjoining field, but in their wild and wary eye there was an unmeasurable spirit, a demon belonging only to their kind.

You must be wondering what had happened to *him* during this chaos. Had he trotted off and married a nice, normal woman, with good culinary interests and not even a canary in her dowry? No. He was there, but convinced now of my insanity. Our snatched moments of passion always ended up with his expressed disapproval of my lifestyle. He obviously still loved the fragment of me which had survived, but breakfast with eight cats and Igor pinching his toast and peeing on his briefcase had become worse than intolerable. Sometimes we talked about distant things, such as the time I flew in a private aircraft to be with him and, looking out from the plane, I could see the tiny airfield and just his car parked nearby. In those heady days, I had become a non-functioning globule of happiness. The tabloids had stopped publishing their bizarre accounts of my divorce and had given up trying to gouge bits of information about my private life out of my friends and colleagues. We had decided to do everything secretly. This, of course, added to the pathos and romance of it. It was our golden time, and now further on into my life its memory was the fragile thread which held us together.

'You're not the same person I knew,' he said. Sorrow the cat made off with his toast. 'You have become animal crazy.' Daniel the parrot threw his seed box to the bottom of the cage, so he had to repeat the accusation. I was growing tired of justifying myself to people, and the disappointment was that I had hoped I would never have to do it with him.

'I can't explain,' I said wearily. 'It's my calling. It's my passion.' I banged my fist on the table. 'So I like being with animals, for God's sake. Is this some sort of crime?'

Igor quickly put himself to bed and all eight cats shot into the hall. Their exit was made more noticeable because they took a short cut across the breakfast table, and for one moment, even I could see his dilemma.

'Fine, fine,' he said, 'obviously we can't talk about this. I'd better go.'

'You're always *going*,' I shrieked.

'You're always giving me cause to go!' he yelled.

'I need support.'

'Then get *them* to give it to you.'

He pointed to the two tortoises basking under their lamp by the Aga, which because of their natural sloth-like nature had not joined in the previous exodus. I began to collect the breakfast dishes, hurling them into the sink, and he went upstairs to get dressed. Igor had devoured his socks. He threaded his feet into the remains, tipped a sleeping cat out of his briefcase and left through the back door, slamming it behind him. One by one the animals returned. Igor was first. He rested his blond silk head on my knee and offered a soft high-pitched whine. Soon I was surrounded by eyes and silence and a kind of 'waiting'. Daniel crouched on his water dish. He sensed the return of order, but just to make sure of his position he said in his best baby-doll voice, 'I'm your sweetheart.'

Our quarrels were different now. It was harder to grieve, and instead of walking around with a stone on my chest I knew I could wait until the next time the phone rang.

'Hello – it's me.'

'Hello me.'

'Are you all right?'

'I'm fine. And you?'

'Yes, I suppose so.'

'When you slammed the door the other night a picture fell off the wall.'

'Oh, darling, I'm sorry.'

'It's all right – just telling you.' A long 'don't know what to say next' pause. 'Anyway, I'll see you.'

'See you.'

'Bye.'

'Bye.'

Oh, God's curse on the man! If only he would say something unforgivable, if only he would exchange brevity and mystique for honest-to-goodness male ranting (I'm shouting now). If only he had never been there.

Gone

You almost made me love you,
With your secret look and your boy's hair,
But something moved behind your smile.
Was she still there?

You always denounced her,
With your trembling lip
And your practised shrug,
But it was there in your eye,
The lie.

I'm glad I didn't show it,
The gathering joy – the looking forward,
The waiting for the end of a traitor's smile,
And in its place – a lover's sigh.
And now it has come – she has truly gone.
But so have I.

When I sat watching the rehearsal of *Luv*, seeing Michael Angelis, a truly loved friend as well as a fine actor, glancing through his lines and singing the very tune I sang as I wrote them I remembered him in *The Liver Birds*. It was in my earliest days of television. I had not yet earned respect or trust. I sat in the little nest of low esteem and the stars pecked away at my scripts whenever they felt the urge. Michael had been cast as Lucien, the rabbit-loving man of the family. I felt as if I was building a character that nobody would ever understand and that I would have to be content with the actor's interpretation. And then suddenly he spoke. He had grasped every aspect of the man I had in mind: the slow, deadpan delivery, the sheer pathos when he spoke of the creatures he was obsessed with and, in spite of the flat, Liverpool tones, the captured humour lurking behind it. I remembered thinking, if this is writing for television, it's easy. But I soon found out that for the new and fearful writer, creating for television is not like that. Often it is almost impossible to convey the sound in your brain at the moment of writing: a different voice, a different intonation, someone else's version of what you know so well knocks you off that safe rock of confidence and you find yourself abandoning your own thoughts and swimming like hell for the nearest shore – that being how the actor thinks it should be done.

They were trouble-filled days, and they lasted for a long time. Then came the time when my script had been brutally readjusted to suit everyone's needs. I spoke up. The normal, feeble little twitter had taken on serious proportions and, trembling inside, I faced the cast and the producer.

'That's not how I saw it,' I said.

A thousand aghast faces surrounded me. It was as if they had forgotten I was there and I had come up through the floorboards threatening them with my bat's wings and my scorpion tail.

'How did you see it?' asked the producer.

The problem then was that I didn't know how I saw it. All clarity had left. Polly James and Nerys Hughes were *stars*, and I was a northern hick pretending to be a writer.

'It should be sad at this point,' I said.

They were moving in on me. 'We're doing comedy,' the producer said.

I was outwitted. I had come into a world I didn't understand. Everybody seemed to be an intellectual.

They spoke of their days at RADA, their nights in the theatre, famous names were their closest friends and they had tea at the Ritz. I fled from the rehearsal rooms and hailed a taxi. Ten minutes later I was headbutting my way into the Head of Comedy's office.

'Carla, my darling! How are you?' He rose from behind his desk and came to hug me. 'Sit down. Let me get you some coffee.' I was wearing black as usual, with matching mascara heading towards my cheekbones. 'You look wonderful. How's the series?'

'I'm going home,' I replied.

'Home! My darling, why?'

'I don't like being a writer. I don't understand the people.'

'But you've got a smash hit series. You've won an award. You can't go home. I'll speak to them.'

Whilst he was asking his secretary to put him through to the rehearsal rooms I fled for the second time, and on the train to Liverpool the depression suddenly turned to triumph. I had uttered a protest, and when it came to needing the next script someone would have to acknowledge my existence. That thought itself gave me the strength to go back to the tiled cell they call a kitchen, and the nothingness of the suburban road in which I used to live.

Several days later I was on the train again, this time going back to London. The Head of Comedy, the producer and both Nerys and Polly had phoned me. They had been charming and friendly. I wore my pseudo arrogance for as long as I could before I relented. The young man in the opposite seat on the train spoke to me round about Stafford.

'You look very thoughtful,' he said.

'Yes,' I admitted.

'What do you do?'

'I'm a writer,' I said. It felt a bit nearer the truth now.

'What do you write?'

'Comedy,' I said.

A little 'Oh' escaped his lips. It was a very unimpressed 'Oh' – one I was to encounter often. I knew that if I had said I wrote drama, he would have leapt to his feet and insisted on buying me coffee, he would have carried my case and pleaded for my telephone number. Instead he crouched behind his newspaper and dematerialized somewhere near Nuneaton.

The worry clouds were overhead now. *Luv* was not doing well. The ratings were low and I was aware that the BBC had paid me a lot of money. A mixture of guilt and bewilderment beset me. I had a work force at the sanctuary building animal units and aviaries. People had started to appear at the gate with little boxes and the crumpled contents often meant a veterinary bill of anything between thirty and eighty pounds – and most of the animals were irreversibly injured, which meant they had to live out their lives at the sanctuary. And that meant more units, more heating, more food. Within five months the upkeep of it, including paltry wages for the workers, came to nearly a thousand pounds a week.

Fundraising was the obvious thing, but it wasn't easy. People seeing my name on the information sheet automatically assumed that I was rich, especially as my friends Rita Tushingham was a director and Linda McCartney was a patron. Slowly my resources were diminishing and the shocking thought that if should I die the whole project would finish kept me awake at nights. My story-telling mind kept presenting me with dreadful scenarios. The tabloids, as usual, played a pre-dominant role: 'Carla's ark sinks', 'Scriptwriter's rescued animals need rescuing'. I wondered who on earth could manage Hector, the brain-damaged pigeon, Amy the flightless and featherless, and Daisy, the partly paralysed. Who could tend them the way we did? Who would hand feed them and then exercise them in their special slings four times a day? Who would remember to switch the heating on in the units? Who would be mad enough to put Nature's mishaps on the list of impor-tance? As I wrestled with this panic an even bigger one came. Because Broadhurst Manor had been trans-ferred from my company to my own name, I was ren-dered liable for an immediate high tax bill plus Capital

Gains Tax from the year 1973. The figure came to more than I had earned in a year – and it cleaned me out completely. The only thing I could do was to start a grave cutting-down process. This had to begin in the house as there was no way I could make savings on the sanctuary.

My first big gesture was to charge outside and disconnect the floodlights which trained on the manor at night, next to turn down the central heating and switch off other lights when not in use. Two of my much-valued helpers had to go, and eventually I turned my attention to the barns and the yards which also had floodlights. Finally, the once yellow-bathed buildings were plunged into darkness. We went about the task of keeping the animals warm and fed whilst we ourselves were cold and tired. In the long, dark corridors of the house we were colliding with each other, and as the only rooms fully heated were those we actually lived in, at five o'clock my bedroom filled up with cats and dogs fighting for a place by the heated pipes.

Accompanying the growing doom was the knowledge that the ratings for *Luv* were still going down – mainly, I suspect, because we were opposite *The Bill*, which is a tremendously popular programme. This lethal concoction of all things going wrong followed me into the spring – a time I had not yet experienced at Broadhurst. The joys of waking up to the sound of the

surrounding fields and woodlands were tainted by the
fear of perhaps having to give it up, but at least there
were more light hours and gradually the warmth of
summer came. The tall oaks and chestnut trees unfolded
their splendour and created a canopy of green over the
crimson and yellow azalea bushes. The lakes sent up
sharp shoots of bulrushes where dragonflies hovered
silently and toads crouched with new young stomachs
to fill. Now and then, the startling brilliant blue of the
kingfisher would dart across the water and the lone
peach-coloured Koyp fish would loll about just beneath
the surface whilst the frenetic roach twisted and leapt
around him.

In spite of the uncertainty, these were truly magic
days, punctuated by the success we were having with
our animals. Like Fred, the duck, who had been savaged
by a dog. When he came to us, the rip in his back had
exposed his lungs. Karen and Peter went automatically
into the routine of preparing a bed in the hospital room
and putting a heat pad in place. Shock is usually the
killer in these cases, but little Fred was still with us the
following morning. Gently we gave him some lectade,
which is a nutritional solution, and it was time to call
Alan Jones, our vet. It took seventy-one stitches to
mend the wound. Fred could not bend his neck, so he
had to walk upright. He looked rather like a feathered
stick on legs. Gradually we progressed him from the

hospital room to a stable, to an outside unit, to one of the lakes where he became a proper duck again.

Mr Crow had been shot in the eye. He sat on our yard gate with his head hanging low between his feet and his crop shrivelled and empty. For two weeks he hovered between being dead and being deranged. The psychological effect of the sudden loss of half his sight was far more life threatening than the actual wound. We built him a special unit with a cabin which had logs and leaves in it, and after a while we put Hopsy, the one-legged crow, in with him. He had also been shot, not once but twice. They will never be real crows again, but the blue light had come back into Mr Crow's eye and they ate and bathed and their heads were high. Our task now was to overshadow their terrifying experience and to make their limited life free from recall.

Chapter 12

Stray Dog

I took him on a lead,
He wasn't mine,
Though he chose my doorstep on which to
   whine.
I looked in all directions,
Avoided eye connections,
Then took him to the dogs' home and filled in the
   form about him.
Male – young – no collar –
And I walked away.
He wasn't mine.

In the yard, I hesitated,
I could hear his loneliness,
Sense the scars of other times.
I closed the metal gates and I heard keys turn.
His wail was lost now,
Gone to join the rest.

Oh God, why me,
Why not next door or Number Nine?

The following day, I looked through the bars –
That was it – he was mine.

And so back to the gathering clouds. I awoke one morning with the strange feeling that there was a door open somewhere. I could feel the chilly morning air greeting me as I went down the staircase, and then I found a small ornament on the floor in the hall. The cats have been messing about, I thought, but when I got to the main lounge it was clear that the house had been burgled. Prior to this I had been visited by my insurance people who inspected the manor and issued a document setting out the things I must do to make the place secure. Every lock and bolt and 'anti-enter' device ever invented was poised for action. A bulldozer could not have got through any of my doors. The tall front gates were electrified, if a moth dared to fly across a room the resulting clang would have rendered the entire population of Sussex with acute ear problems and there were nine dogs scattered over the estate – and yet, there it was: a tiny hole cut in the window just big enough to put a hand through and open up a frame of it. Because there were seven people in the house at the time, I had not needed to set the alarms, so the burglars managed to creep into every room and take everything which would easily pass through the window space. This included my beautiful clock collection, most of my silver and a host of other trinkets. Fortunately, my pictures were too big – except for one, and they dropped that in the garden. Not one dog barked, not one bang did anyone hear. Instead of confronting the Fort Knox of the front of the house they had come across the fields and prised their way through the vulnerable back of it, and little did I know when I got up in the night to let a mewing cat into my bedroom that they were downstairs helping themselves. It was at that point my hooligan lurcher had opened his eyes and blinked. He then strolled to the bedroom door and gave a very laid-back if not inaudible growl. I told him to shut up, which he gladly did and collapsed back into his bed.

Reluctantly the BBC requested more *Luv*. The first series had faded off the screens leaving little more than a puff of interest. This was new to me, and if it hadn't been for the support of Michael Angelis and Sue Johnston, who told me that they were proud to be in it and promptly signed up for the second series, I might have come apart at this point. I decided to go and spend my birthday with my mother. It was a strange feeling I had. Something urged me to abandon the problems and go to her.

We spent two days giggling and wandering together. I drove her round the places she enjoyed and as we parked in Bold Street, with a sandwich and a cup of coffee, I suddenly saw in that lovely face a transparent paleness. Her smile seemed too big, her voice sounded tired – but all three disappeared as quickly as they came, and I thought that it was an image created by my own dread rather than reality.

Two days later she was in hospital. Things were going wrong in her stomach, but there was nothing definite. She was being sick the whole time, and in between she paused to give some stick to the nurse who had handed her a cardboard container. 'Is this the best you can do? You expect me to be sick in that? I'm used to cut glass.'

After staying by her for three days and nights, she decided to die whilst I was out of the ward. She didn't like to display anything which spelled weakness, and it would be right for her to be alone then. I sat for a long time, touching her face, her arms, her tiny busy little hands with traces of pale pink nail varnish on and an assortment of rings and bracelets which the family had bought her over the years.

I couldn't cry somehow, and I became obsessed with closing her mouth because I knew she would not like being seen like that. Wide black bruises were appearing on her arms where they had put in the drip. I covered them for her, and when I looked at her for the last time a terrible scream was locked in my chest. When I closed the flowered curtains to leave, I opened them again to make sure that she didn't mind me going. The little old lady in the next bed called to rescue me: 'I'm sorry, luv, I'm so sorry.' We clasped hands and I remember thinking that my mother had never looked as fragile as she did. The other patients were sleeping, and as I walked out into the dawn I wanted to go back to the curtain again – maybe my mother was sleeping too.

Outside a thunderstorm had started and as I drove away, I recalled reading that Beethoven had died during a thunderstorm. I envisaged my mother with him, and in her usual unguarded way saying what she had always said when she saw pictures of him. 'Your music is as bad-tempered as your face.'

The day before the funeral, my brother Ramon phoned and asked me to go to the chapel of rest with him. I didn't want to. I had had those moments behind the hospital curtains.

'I think we should,' he said; then, bringing in his unique way of dealing with things, he added, 'She won't like it if we don't. You know how she is.'

Her left eye was slightly open, and it was still shining. They had somehow altered her face. She looked as if she was about to tell us off. Ramon walked around the coffin, then stood at the end of it and smiled at her. 'Well, Hive, you've burned your last kettle.'

'She did her ninth one in last week,' I said.

'Did you hear that? Nine kettles! And how many hearing aids have you lost?'

'Four,' I said.

'Four,' emphasized Ramon. 'You'll have to behave when you get up there, you know.'

We both broke into a whispered laughter and in this mood I recalled a well-loved incident. I had left her sitting in the Range Rover which was parked in a forbidden place. When I came out of the shop three multi-coloured police cars had surrounded it. Because it was raining heavily, a waiting policeman guided me into one of the police cars and there I sat on the back seat with a burly officer on either side of me, a gathering crowd around us, radios going and lights flashing. As they questioned my lunatic parking, a knock came on the car window. Her bright little face appeared and she mouthed the words, 'I'm just going for a loaf.' Ramon and I laughed – in fact it seemed to me now that all three of us were laughing, and after more reminiscing and with a parting touch Ramon and I went to the car park. 'She'll be all right,' said Ramon, and we waved to each other as we drove through the iron gate. All the way back I kept thinking what a truly nice man my brother is.

The funeral now over I flew back home. I left her flat in Claremont exactly as it was. Something vital had left my life. Not just the 'Mother' or the friend, but the irreplaceable light. Everything I would do from then on would be entwined with her approval and her spirit. Now I was forced to remember the rule that someone had laid down: The show must go on – and so it must.

My mother's death brought much warmth from my friends. Letters and phone calls were plenty, kind words flowed, but a deadline is a deadline and as soon as I got home I had to write, of all things, comedy. It reminded me of the desperate time when my little grandson, Arragorn, was drowned in the River Mersey. He had been missing for a month and they had found his body. The house in Liverpool was crowded with police and divers and reporters, and amidst all this came a phone call from *The Liver Birds* office.

'Carla, darling, is that you?'

'Oh, hello. Yes, it's me.'

'It's about scene six, darling, page twenty-nine. That speech about Mrs Hutchin's hat – you know – "She's always got either a salad or a dead bird on her head".'

Something in my brain switched off and mechanically I replied, 'Oh yes, I know the one.'

'Could you give Sandra an extra line so that she can get out of the room without there being a gap?'

'Yes, I'll phone it through to you in a minute.'

'Thank you, darling. Everything all right?'

'It's fine – yes. Everything's fine.'

A funny line arrived on the page and I rang it through. It was at times like this that I believed talent was twinned with insanity.

So why do I write? It's because I can't seem to shut up, basically. The moment a thought enters my head I have to yell about it. For instance, I am sitting on a train to Liverpool and I see a dead sheep in a field. My immediate thought is when will I die? Will it be in a minute, before I have finished this deliberation? I hope not, because there is hardly anybody in sight, especially the first-class compartment where I imagine members of the medical profession would be should I need them. The only people nearby are two men who are discussing loudly the imperfections of their mutual colleague who has peeved them severely by being happy with his work and at peace with his wife. Should I suddenly gasp and fall into my Maxpax coffee, I doubt if they would notice because the conversation is moving excitedly towards their own marriages, which over the years seem to have sapped them of that human ingredient called 'goodwill to all men and possibly expiring women'.

Ideally I would prefer to die during a glorious moment. Receiving the OBE would have been ideal because my family were all there in the gallery, the band was playing suitably stricken music and I am sure the Queen would have summoned her best doctors.

And because nothing tatty is seen to leave the Palace, I would have been dispatched rather stylishly to cold storage. It would be disastrous if the event happened in my own bed, since being found with rejuvenating gel over my face and 'works while you slumber' body oil bonding me to the bedclothes would give the tabloids too much of a tasty scoop. Whereas if I were suddenly to slump over a supermarket trolley, the slight advantage would be that I would inadvertently publicize the cause of vegetarianism.

Fifteen years ago I did embrace death. I was having my appendix out and was administered a wrong injection which seized up my central nervous system and shut down my ability to breathe. I won't attempt to describe the ensuing nightmare, except to say that someone finally noticed that my face had taken on a navy blue appearance, which resulted in various alarm bells ringing and my eventual resuscitation.

But what of that journey, so often described as 'going towards a golden light with a feeling of omnipotent knowledge'? My experience was obviously reserved for those going down and not up. A great fire broke out in my brain. I felt angry because I was halfway through a series and I didn't want anyone else to finish it. I wanted to kiss and hug my family and plead with them not to fight over my assets, and not to let my dog off the lead because he was paranoid about German Shepherds. Most

177

disappointing of all was that up to the point where death and I touched fingers, there was no sign of that bearded man who I was told as a child would be waiting for me with outstretched hands and all the sweets I could eat. Instead there was blackness and panic and amongst it the irritating thought that when my family arrived that night a quiet-voiced doctor would greet them solemnly and say, 'I'm sorry, she died under the anaesthetic.'

Lying on a starched bed with loved ones placed like pawns and kings around me does not appeal either. Muted voices whispering things like, 'You go and have a coffee, I'll stay with her', or 'You go home and get some sleep' – words designed to make me feel in my last moments an encumbrance. Worst of all would be the tearstained face. There's always one: not family or friend, but the distant relative – the one you can't stand, the one who can't stand you – who suddenly bursts out of the chrysalis, eager to enjoy the ride in a big black car and the tea and fruit cake later.

So how, then, should I die? Certainly with some make-up on, and if it's a windy day and I'm going to be manhandled by a first aid enthusiast, I'd prefer to be wearing my Janet Reger knickers. Although the venue is of some importance, I suppose the criterion is dignity. I don't want to flump or flip or crash or burst into someone's conversation clutching my chest and gurgling.

A quiet closing of the eyes and a Mona Lisa smile would do, or an exit like that of one of my fans. He was sitting on a cosy settee watching television. In her letter his wife wrote, 'My husband turned to me and said, "I'll make supper later. I don't want to miss Carla Lane's stuff."' They were his last words.

As I sat waiting for *him* to visit Broadhurst Manor I was remembering his first visit to Zoffany House. He wandered from room to room.

'It's beautiful, darling.'

'Thank you.' (Igor has his nose in his pocket.)

'We're going to have beads and lace again, are we?' (He was being tender. My heart was jumping. What does it matter? I'll paint the place any bloody colour he likes. Orange if he wants it. There was a sudden change of atmosphere.)

'What has that dog got now?'

'Don't call him "that dog".'

'All right, all right.' (Nicely.) 'What has your dog got now?'

'Your glasses.'

'Oh, shit!'

'He won't harm them.' (I was lying. He went to take them. Igor got down on his elbows and wagged his tail.) There was a crunchy sound – I think it came from the spectacle case.

'Come here!'

'Don't shout.' (Dog and man disappeared through the door.)

I heard them in the lounge, in the hall, in the kitchen and, finally, in the garden.

Outside people were strolling, lovers were smiling at each other. One young man stopped and took a blossom off my quince tree and handed it to his girl. Everything seemed so simple for them. This was my new house. *He* had come to have dinner. *I* was wearing my most disgraceful blouse. *He* had a little present for me sticking out of his pocket. *I* had a bean casserole in the oven. So why was he strangling my dog in the garden?

Suddenly the bell was ringing. The iron gates of Broadhurst were opening. Igor was racing to meet him. Soon he was wandering from room to room.

'It's beautiful, darling.'

'Thank you.'

'What colour are you doing the hall?'

'Geranium.' (There's that wince again.) 'You're wincing.'

'I'm not.'

'You are, I saw you.'

'I'm not.'

'You always wince when I say geranium or green.'

We stand by the fireplace, taking turns to sigh. 'I'm sorry,' he says.

'It's all right,' I say. (Oh God, that face. This is it. I don't care any more.) 'I love you.'

'You're not bad, either.' (I had blown it. He looked frightened.)

'I don't mean ... real love ... you know, all-consuming love, don't-ever-leave-me love, possessive love.' (I'm running out of adjectives.) 'Marry-me love. I don't mean that.'

(He ruffled my hair, then suddenly he kissed me — long and hard. There was something urgent about it. It was different. I was dying of joy.)

'Good,' he said.

Grandchildren

I try to keep them a secret, but they couldn't
keep me a secret.

1 The very grown-up grandaughter, Ivana – suddenly
   leapt from childhood to something lethal.

2 Hannah and Danielle, Nigel's children.

3 The very eccentric grandaughter, Romana, Carl's
   daughter.

4 Aeneas in Canada with the seals just after taking his
   degree. He is now a Marine Biologist.

5 De Vona, Carl's daughter, the most grown-up
   grandaughter of all. Oh God, I feel so old!

Afterword

It is still dark. I am tossing and turning. The grey pillow of my mind is frantic with thoughts. I've finished the book – nobody will want to read it – what next? Another series, a film, a play, a letter to John Major about the live transportation of animals?

Dear Mr Major

I am at Shoreham along with three hundred other protesters. Listen to us – listen to how we feel.

There is complete silence. The long grey road is empty. The traffic has been diverted. We know the trucks are coming. It is during this pause that each one of us has time to reflect on why we are here. Some of us are simply ashamed of our disgraceful years of indifference. Some are re-living the videos of indescribable cruelty to animals. Others are there because the sight of the trucks brought unsurmountable passion to their hearts. As for me, I am rejoicing – I no longer feel alone. I am recalling the endless meetings with ever-changing ministers, sitting in dark brown offices with their polished tables and armoured walls, beating my chest with sorrow and watching them fall into an 'Oh God, not her again' slumber. At the end of twenty years I managed to headbutt my way into Downing Street. The occupant wore a brighter robe of intellect – but the message fled along the same path and into the same vacuum.

There is a cry from the crowd, 'THEY ARE COMING!' One can feel reasoning rise from the crowd and fly like a great escaping bird. All that awaits the trucks now is a kind of anger. The fluorescent-jacketed police tighten their ranks. They wrap around us like a huge yellow rope. We can see them change from men to policemen. At this point, they are to me comforting. I am afraid of violence. Getting hit on the head is an unfavour-ite thought and, just to make sure that they remember my fear, I joke with the immediate ones about my capped teeth – 'For God's sake, don't knock them out – I had to take out a bank loan to have them fixed!' I raise my loudhailer as the steel procession comes nearer. I have no idea what I am going to shout. The people further up the street are already crowding around the police escort.

Some have simply offered themselves to the great wheels of the trucks. I cling to the shoulder of a chosen policeman. I don't really want to die – but I am seeing now the men at the wheels. Their faces seem carved in evil and there is this bleating and squealing. The refined businessman behind me is already shouting, 'Bastards – you barbaric bastards.' There is a violent shifting of the crowd. I am lost in sadness at the sight of dark eyes, the tips of ears, the saliva-covered noses. Suddenly I break through . . . I run towards the truck . . . I want to touch one of the animals – that's all. The big wheels don't frighten me any more. I am filled with the belief that I can stop the truck. Someone tries to pull me away, but I have developed a super strength. I feel into the slats – a warm face, a rough tongue licking my fingers. I want to explain to him that we are putting him through this anguish to save the rest of his kind. Now I am being dragged back to the barriers. It isn't at all painful, only the frustration is painful. I go with the crowd, amongst the sea of banners. My throat is hurting as I shout to the drivers, 'Tell your children what you do! Murderers! Hitler did this to the Jews! Shame on You!'

The rest join in, 'Shame on You! Shame on You! Shame on You!'

Even as we trail off, the siege is over – the trucks go through. A bedraggled mass of us stand helplessly. Men and women sob openly and, from the children's safe area, we hear 'No, Mummy – No! No!'

The police have cast their yellow rope again. With reasoning still gone, we cannot understand as we look at them why these men to whom we usually run for protection are now hitting us – when we are calling for something human and commendable. Some of the crowd throw abuse towards them – 'Fascists!' 'Bastards!' 'Scum!' But really we know that they are just doing a job and that they are with us, which brings their dilemma into the same bewilderment as our own.

And so we stand, another layer of anger lining our guts. Here and there are skirmishes. From the heap of bobble caps and sweaters and bright police jackets, somebody's grandmother is lifted. She kicks out and at the same time tries to keep her skirt down over her knees. One of her shoes comes off. She is deposited beside the barrier and, after wiping her eyes and abandoning the other shoe, she goes back in. Protesters and police are caught in the cat-like stare that precedes a fight – fists landing on chests and backs – screaming – swearing – there is no comforting voice for any of us. And amidst all this, a little lady, bent forward, her bony hands pitting her banner against a howling wind. It reads 'Hang Lacey by the Bollocks!' A man who has just recovered from a stroke has written his scream on a large sheet. The wind distorts his message so he shouts it painfully to the passing motorists, who beep in acknowledgement. A young girl stands at the intersection. She has got her banner the wrong way round – she is unwittingly showing a Heinz Beans advert; and, down at the shore, the riot squad is pursuing some of the more adventurous protesters across the sand. We cheer them as they run towards the sea. There is nothing they can do, the red ship of shame is far out. The police outnumber them three to one, but on they go, to the chants of the crowd, 'Yes! Yes! Go For It! Yes! Yes!' One by one, they are brought down and hustled into the vans – and we turn our plea to the motorists again. Residents close their windows. Police wince as I leap about with my dreaded loudhailer. Motorists beep loud and long as they pass. Their noise becomes the Song of Shoreham. At the end of seven cold, hungry, tired hours of waiting, their acclaim is all we have left.

So why? Why do we do this? The man in the expensive suit; the lady in the very proper camel coat; the young man with the balaclava; the old, old lady who gets a lift from our tolerant police and brings her zimmer frame with her; the ordinary anoraked folk of Britain. Is it because of those dark places where cruelty reigns, where people make money being cruel – which until the Compassion in World Farming videos were unknown to us? Is it because we are educated by them and we know now how meat gets on our plate? Or is it the arrival of mistrust, the loss of faith in the pinstripe-suited men of power who speak of nothing but the Maastricht Treaty and its free trade? Is it that now we have to ask Brussels for permission not to be cruel? And is it because these men are distant from the people, the ordinary people – who care about things like their children, their dogs, their fields, their streams, their planet – and now the animals which share it and embellish it?

We are asked by the defender of this vile trade to think about the drivers and their jobs. Our answer is: 'You knew when you bought your truck what you were doing. It is built for what you are doing. You chose cruelty.' We are asked to understand the farmers. Our answer is: 'You are spoiled with your grants and your subsidies and your set-asides – and now you want to make money out of what you yourselves call the debris of your farmyards as well as from the milk the grief-stricken mother gives you.' We are asked to listen to Mr Waldegrave. Our answer is: 'We don't believe him.' We are asked to wait for the Government to battle with Brussels. Ou answer is: 'You are battling for the wrong things. We don't want travelling time reduced; we don't want open sheds instead of crates; we don't want animals to leave our shores and go to the desensitized men of other countries, who wait with their screwdrivers and their sledgehammers and who never have and never will obey the human rule. We don't want any animal of any kind to go to this indescribable nightmare.'

And so – with the not condoned but understood emotions of the young man who shattered the windscreen of the first truck through Shoreham, there came a new skyline for the animals, a new hope for the protesters. The steel procession, exporters, police, the money makers seemed not impenetrable after all. The following day, ministers mumbled, supermarkets shifted uncomfortably – a new thinking enveloped the sleeping minds of the meat eaters. Perhaps something in our gut reminds us that this is a bad world and that the human being is not all he should be. And perhaps, as we sit round the deathbed of our violent planet, our spirits seem to be in need of purity – and animals are the only pure things we have left.

Please hear us, Mr Major.

For and on behalf of the protesters.

I know what brought all that on. Recently I visited a local school for backward children. They smiled and talked and touched my hair. Their plight reminded me of the creatures in my sanctuary – the creatures in the trucks, the factory farms, the laboratories – innocent and brave, handicapped by a vindictive mood of fate, the quality of their existence measured only by the care we choose to give them. Those of us who realize this must scream and shout for all creatures. We must not question our cause – it will rise above greed. We owe it to them as we go around unharmed and safe in our own completeness.

And so, on I go, into the limbo of life – what becomes of me lies up there where the clouds gather and disperse.

But when I go to the field gate and give a low whistle to bring in Joe the crow, and when I touch his magnificent blackness and see his blue police-lamp eyes blinking with trust, I know I am looking at the answer to the question 'Why do you do it?'

Photograph Credits

The Author and publishers would like to thank the following people and organizations for permission to reproduce photographs in this book. All photos other than those listed below have been provided by the Author from her own collection.

PAGES 40 AND 41
1. *Daily Mirror* (Manchester). 4. *Evening Standard.* 5. Christopher Richardson. 6. Christopher Richardson. 9. Christopher Richardson.

PAGES 70 AND 71
1. BBC. 2. BBC. 3. *Daily Mirror.* 4. BBC. 5. People in Pictures. 7. Studios. 8. BBC. 9. BBC.

PAGES 100 AND 101
2. Peter Hogan. 7. Meridian. 9. *Radio Times.*